POEMS OF PROTEST OLD AND NEW

Poems of Protest Old and New

A Selection of Poetry

EDITED, WITH AN INTRODUCTION, BY

Arnold Kenseth

The Macmillan Company, New York

Collier-Macmillan Ltd., London

Library of Congress Catalog Card Number: 68-19820

FIRST PRINTING

The Macmillan Company, New York
Collier-Macmillan Canada Ltd., Toronto, Ontario

Printed in the United States of America

Acknowledgment is made to the following for permission to reprint from previously published material:

The Publishers and the Trustees of Amherst College for "What Soft, Cherubic Creatures" from Thomas H. Johnson, Editor, *The Poems of Emily Dickinson*. Cambridge, Mass.: The Belknap Press of Harvard University Press, Copyright, 1951, 1955, by the President and Fellows of Harvard College.

Appleton-Century, affiliate of Meredith Press, for "The Flower-Fed Buffaloes" from *Going to the Stars*, by Vachel Lindsay, Copyright, 1926, by D. Appleton & Co. Copyright renewed, 1954, by Elizabeth C. Lindsay.

Sterling A. Brown for "Strong Men" from *Southern Road*, Harcourt, Brace & World, 1932.

David R. Clark and *The Kenyon Review* for "Asylum," summer 1955 *Kenyon Review*. Copyright © 1955 by Kenyon College.

Doubleday & Co., Inc., for "Dolor," copyright 1943 by Modern Poetry Association, Inc., from *The Collected Poems of Theodore Roethke*.

Dorothy Durem for "Award" by Ray Durem from *Poets of Today: A New American Anthology*, ed. Walter Lowenfels.

Norma Millay Ellis for Edna St. Vincent Millay's "Dirge Without Music" from *Collected Poems*, Harper & Row. Copyright 1928, 1955 by Edna St. Vincent Millay and Norma Millay Ellis.

"Plaint" by Charles Henry Ford, from *Modern Verse in English*, eds. David Cecil and Allen Tate. New York: The Macmillan Company, 1958.

Harry Fox Agency for Tom Paxton's "We Didn't Know," Copyright 1965 by Deep Fork Music, Inc.

Grove Press, Inc., for Edward Field's "Unwanted" from *Stand Up, Friend, with Me*, Copyright © 1963 by Edward Field.

Harcourt, Brace & World, Inc., for "i sing of Olaf," Copyright 1931, 1959 by E. E. Cummings from his *Poems 1923–1954* and

For the Front Four

ELAINE   BRUCE

GEOFFREY   EVAN

CONTENTS

x

xi

INTRODUCTION

We are in a decade, perhaps an age, when all sorts and conditions of men are rising up to protest (declare against) all sorts and conditions in our human situation. Everywhere, the "have-nots" are challenging the "haves"; the morally awake are prodding the indifferently asleep; the impatient are threatening the patient; both the Left and the Right are attacking the Center; the new thinks that it despises the old. In a well-worn sense, "whatever is" is wrong. The current traitor is the middle class, and treason is gradually being defined as the liberal view. The choice offered seems to be between either a soma-soaked brotherly "happening" with Whirl as benevolent king or the orderly, albeit vicious, tyranny of Orwell's 1984. Within our own borders the arenas are brimming and booming: inner city ghettos, rural slums, local draft boards, P.T.A. committees, factories exuding smog, churches gathering affluence, campuses and coffee houses, Selma and Cicero, the Mississippi Delta and the cities of Detroit and Newark, nuclear test sites and pornographic paperbacks. Under attack are segregation, the war in Vietnam, control of the universities, inequalities in selective service, Christian hypocrisies, second-class citizenship, white collar culture, poverty, river pollution, and the BOMB. The ways of protest seem both strangely new and familiarly old; boycotts, sit-ins, marches, voter registration, letters to the editor or congressman, signed advertisements, white papers, documentary films, propaganda movies, TV exposés, panel discussions, and so on. Similarly, the protesters are various and, interestingly, often on opposite sides. Though the majority of college students remain laissez-faire and security-haunted (like their parents), an aroused and morally sensitive cluster of beatniks and Ivy Leaguers seek redress of grievances not only for themselves but also for the undernourished and the underprivileged across the land. Nuns, ministers, and rabbis march with folk singer and atheist under the gunfire of klansmen and the anathema of Birchites and bishops. Worried mothers gulp as Johnny's guitar sounds louder, his hair grows longer, and *Rock* rolls into "frug." "Death of God" theologians, Black Power advocates, topless waitresses, LSD tasters, high school dropouts, peace corps workers, "hippies," columnists, minutemen, college professors who "teach-in" are all, after their fashion, declaring against something. And not the least among the princes of protest is the poet.

Thus, one intention of this anthology of "protest poems" is to acknowledge the currency of protest in this present time by offering a sampling of immediately contemporary poets who take up one or another of the cries against some wrong still to be set right in America or in the world.

A second purpose of this book, however, is to recall that man is perennially a "protester" and to point out that most of the matters spoken against in our decade (and century) have been dealt with, time and again, throughout man's stunning and stormy history—and noticeably dealt with by poets. To show this repetition, I have, in most instances, placed an older poem side by side with a new one on the same subject: for example, lines from Aeschylus' *Agamemnon* decrying the waste of young Greek lives at Troy with Edgar Lee Masters' "Harry Wilmans," a poem citing the horrors of the Spanish American War; Donne's famous "Death Be Not Proud" opposite Dylan Thomas' "Do Not Go Gentle into That Good Night"; or William Blake's "London," which sets "the chimney sweeper's cry," beside Stephen Spender's picture of the dismal evils of "An Elementary School Class Room in a Slum." Read in such parallel, these poems underscore that in certain basic human relations—the waste of war, the mortality of man and its meaning, the oppression of the poor —we have not advanced much farther than the early Hebrews or the Greeks either in our morality or our wisdom. Even what appears to be a condition new to our time: namely, that mankind and all its history can be totally obliterated because of the Bomb—is a central cry of agony in the verses of the prophet Jeremiah in the year 650 B.C. And man's complaint about being simply mortal man is heard over and over again from the book of Job to the poems of Gerard Manley Hopkins, Thomas Hardy, and the twentieth century poet, Robert Francis. To emphasize these parallels is in no way to deny the need for current protests; but such realization does give chastening perspective in a period when much of the effectiveness of the present attack is diminished because the attackers are reluctant to learn from history.

Since this collection is small (113 poems by 98 authors are represented), the reader will understand that this volume intends to be suggestive rather than inclusive. Most of the poems have been chosen as much for being valid poems as for being examples of protest. Other selections are verses only—their value being that they provide a mode of attack—righteous indignation in rhyme, grievance caught in a strong meter. Throughout, the voices of the poets vary from marked irritation and anger, through sarcasm and irony (tragic and comic) to understated lament and serious grief. "Grievances," writes Frost, "are a form of impatience. Griefs are a form of patience." Possibly, then, another distinction that can be found in this anthology is that the great poem of protest speaks out of an abiding sorrow for what man has done to man. In such a poem, the tone is not petulant or clever, nor does it end up, as do some of our San Francisco poems, in a frenzied self-pitying "howl." Instead, the vast dignity of man —his worth, his mystery, his paradoxical nature—are held in the presence of the very tragedy that cripples or destroys him. Such poems "bring the eternal note of sadness in" and always raise the great questions of man's ultimate meanings. They bear the experience of man not merely as he confronts his problems but as he confronts his nature. They see the world and its human situation *sub specie aeternitatis*—"under the gaze of eternity." For this reason, the true poet may, in the long run, have more to say in fundamental protest to any generation than the part-time propagandist who, after all, is keyed up to shout at the particular enemy before him. But rather than draw lines between the two breeds of outcry, we may more wisely affirm that each emphasis has its own place and usefulness. Some wrongs are so glaring and immediate that only a sarcastic Kingsley Amis or an angry Tom Paxton can cause the casual, usual, safe man to turn and look —and, hopefully, *act:* while Aeschylus, Shakespeare, Blake, Hardy, Hopkins (to list a few of the great ones) require of us that, when we look and when we act, we look deeply and act with a foresight which never forgets the dilemma between ends and means and almost always perceives how the skirmishes for justice in any decade arise out of the ancient war between good and evil.

Some of the poems gathered herein are maverick, possibly anachronistic—either because history has passed their problem by (or so it seems), or because they plead special causes, or because the issues they raise are less demanding of our serious response, or because their language is intentionally light. Henry the Fifth's soliloquy on the lonely role of the king appears outdated, until we recall recent discussions of the heavy burden of ceremony and decision that attends the office of the President of the United States. Ralph Hodgson's plea for mercy "to little hunted hares" sounds sentimental compared to the roaring cadences of Jeremiah—yet not so to the animal lover. Because Americans are often a people almost willingly wasteful of natural resources for the sake of new housing and urban advance, only the man who has thought decades ahead will cry Amen to Stanley Kunitz' "The War Against the Trees." There is a quick, comic bite in the six line poem, "On the Setting Up of Mr. Butler's Monument in Westminster Abbey"—"The poet's fate is here in emblem shown: / He asked for bread, and he received a stone." We shake our heads ruefully; because poets still starve for food and fame . . . in their lifetime.

The strength of poetry as a vehicle of protest is that a well-wrought poem involves us, blood and bone, heart and mind, in the experience providing and provoking the protest. A poem is that use of language and measure which reenacts in the reader what has already happened to the poet. So we shiver in the flesh and in the soul when broken Lear cries out on behalf of the poor, "How shall your houseless heads and unfed sides, / Your loop'd and window'd raggedness, defend you / From seasons such as these?" To be sure, this collection abounds in poems that make direct statements as to what the poem stands against; yet the supportive and organic presence of images bearing color, shape, landscape, person, motion, flight, falling, fire, etc.—supplies a context of quivering and lively senses that are raging quietly or noisily against the particular folly or injustice found in man or his universe. It is this capacity to *embody* (incarnate) protest that gives the poet the advantage over others who decry the times in editorials, letters, placards, the brightest satirical prose. The poet and his poems put us in the peace march, at the hanging tree, inside the skin and bones of the hungry, before the awesome tyranny of the powers and principalities, and under the mushroom burst of the Bomb. The poem does not simply urge: "Think on these things." It pushes us into the fray, into an active "You are here!"

Finally, let it be noted, to protest (stand against) something is to affirm (stand for) something—usually the opposite of what is under attack. The outcry, over the centuries, against war via grievance or grief is a declaration for peace. The several poems smoldering against a meaningless, impersonal universe can persuade us to our need for a God or a wisdom that gives man purpose and place. Cynical, wild, self-righteous, philosophical though their language be—the poets want the hungry fed, the naked clothed, the Negro made a first-class citizen, genuine understanding among nations, the imagination kept free, a whole variety of human failings straightened up and allowed to walk erect with dignity and hope. Poets are as Ezra Pound so rightly described them —"the antennae of the race." They are captured by visions; they desire—if not always the City of God, surely a City of Man. Their cry is Blake's:

> Bring me my bow of burning gold!
>   Bring me my arrows of desire!
> Bring me my spear! O clouds, unfold!
>   Bring me my chariot of fire!
>
> I will not cease from mental fight,
>   Nor shall my sword sleep in my hand,
> Till we have built Jerusalem
>   In England's green and pleasant land.

In the long view, these poems, which rush to tear down the idols, unseat the false judges, overthrow the tyrants, and drive the money changers from the temples, ultimately aim "to build up the waste places" and give to mankind "the garland of joy for the ashes of mourning." Let this anthology so declare!

ARNOLD KENSETH

Amherst, Massachusetts

POEMS OF PROTEST OLD AND NEW

I Sit and Look Out

I SIT AND LOOK out upon all the sorrows of the world,
    and upon all oppression and shame,
I hear secret convulsive sobs from young men at anguish
    with themselves, remorseful after deeds done,
I see in low life the mother misused by her children,
    dying, neglected, gaunt, desperate,
I see the wife misused by her husband, I see the treacherous
    seducer of young women,
I mark the ranklings of jealousy and unrequited love
    attempted to be hid, I see these sights on the earth,
I see the workings of battle, pestilence, tyranny, I see
    martyrs and prisoners,
I observe a famine at sea, I observe the sailors casting lots
    who shall be kill'd to preserve the lives of the rest,
I observe the slights and degradations cast by arrogant persons
    upon laborers, the poor, and upon negroes, and the like;
All these—all the meanness and agony without end I
    sitting look out upon,
See, hear, and am silent.

The End of the World

My anguish, my anguish! I writhe in pain!
    Oh, the walls of my heart!
My heart is beating wildly;
    I cannot keep silent;
For I hear the sound of the trumpet,
    the alarm of war.
Disaster follows hard on disaster,
    the whole land is laid waste.
Suddenly my tents are destroyed,
    my curtains in a moment.
How long must I see the standard,
    and hear the sound of the trumpet?
"For my people are foolish,
    they know me not;
They are stupid children,
    they have no understanding.
They are skilled in doing evil,
    but how to do good they know not."

I looked on the earth, and lo, it was waste and void;
    and to the heavens, and they had no light.
I looked on the mountains, and lo, they were quaking,
    and all the hills moved to and fro.
I looked, and lo, there was no man,
    and all the birds of the air had fled.
I looked, and lo, the fruitful land was a desert,
    and all its cities were laid in ruins
        before the Lord, before his fierce anger.

(JEREMIAH 4:19–26)

In a Surrealist Year

In a surrealist year
               of sandwichmen and sunbathers
                   dead sunflowers and live telephones
   house-broken politicos with party whips
   performed as usual
   in the rings of their sawdust circuses
   where tumblers and human cannonballs
                 filled the air like cries
       when some cool clown
               pressed an inedible mushroom button
 and an inaudible Sunday bomb
              fell down
catching the president at his prayers
                 on the 19th green

   O it was a spring
               of fur leaves and cobalt flowers
   when cadillacs fell thru the trees like rain
       drowning the meadows with madness
while out of every imitation cloud
             dropped myriad wingless crowds
               of nutless nagasaki survivors
   And lost teacups
   full of our ashes
   floated by

3

Let Me Alone

I, then, will not restrain my mouth;
I will speak in the anguish of my spirit;
I will complain in the bitterness of my being.
Am I the sea, or a dragon,
That thou appointest a watch over me?
When I think my couch may comfort me,
Or my bed relieve my complaint,
Then thou dost terrify me by nightmares;
So that I prefer strangling,
Death rather than my bones.
I refuse; I shall not live forever.
Let me alone! For my days are but a breath.
What is man that thou shouldst magnify him,
And shouldst set thy mind upon him,
And shouldst inspect him every morning,
And test him every moment?
How long wilt thou not look away from me,
Nor let me alone till I swallow my saliva?
Have I sinned? What do I unto thee, O thou keeper of man?
Why dost thou make me a target for thyself,
So that I am become a burden to thee?
Why dost thou not forgive my transgression,
And make my guilt to pass away?
For soon I shall lie down in the dust;
And thou wilt search for me, but I shall not be.

(*from* THE BOOK OF JOB)

GERARD MANLEY HOPKINS (1844–89)

No Worst, There Is None

No worst, there is none. Pitched past pitch of grief,
More pangs will, schooled at forepangs, wilder wring.
Comforter, where, where is your comforting?
Mary, mother of us, where is your relief?

My cries heave, herds-long; huddle in a main, a chief
Woe, world-sorrow; on an age-old anvil wince and sing—
Then lull, then leave off. Fury and shrieked "No ling-
ering! Let me be fell: force I must be brief."

O the mind, mind has mountains; cliffs of fall
Frightful, sheer, no-man-fathomed. Hold them cheap
May who ne'er hung there. Nor does long our small
Durance deal with that steep or deep. Here! creep,
Wretch, under a comfort serves in a whirlwind: all
Life death does end and each day dies with sleep.

The God of War

At home the hearth lies in sorrow such as this,
And more; in each house throughout the land of Greece
That sent its dearest to make war beyond the sea,
The brave heart is called to school itself
In slow endurance against
Griefs that strike deep into the bosom:
  Those that were sent away they
  Knew, but now they receive back
  Not the faces they longed to see,
  Only a heap of ashes.
The God of War holds the twin scales of strife,
Cruel gold-changer merchandising men,
Embarking homeward from Troy a heap of dust fire-refined,
Making up its weight in grief,
Shapely vessels laden each
With ashes of a friend.
They mourn and praise them, saying, "He
And *he*, who died a noble death—
All to avenge another man's wife."
It is muttered in a whisper,
And it spreads with growling envy of the sons of Atreus.
  They lie still, the possessors
  Each of a strip of Trojan
  Soil, but the land that hides their fair
  Limbs is a foe and foreign.

       (*from* AGAMEMNON)

Harry Wilmans

I was just turned twenty-one,
And Henry Phipps, the Sunday-school superintendent,
Made a speech in Bindle's Opera House.
"The honor of the flag must be upheld," he said,
"Whether it be assailed by a barbarous tribe of Tagalogs
Or the greatest power in Europe."
And we cheered and cheered the speech and the flag he waved
As he spoke.
And I went to the war in spite of my father,
And followed the flag till I saw it raised
By our camp in a rice field near Manila,
And all of us cheered and cheered it.
But there were flies and poisonous things;
And there was the deadly water,
And the cruel heat,
And the sickening, putrid food;
And the smell of the trench just back of the tents
Where the soldiers went to empty themselves;
And there were the whores who followed us, full of syphilis;
And beastly acts between ourselves or alone,
With bullying, hatred, degradation among us,
And days of loathing and nights of fear
To the hour of the charge through the steaming swamp,
Following the flag,
Till I fell with a scream, shot through the guts.
Now there's a flag over me in Spoon River!
A flag! A flag!

(*from* SPOON RIVER ANTHOLOGY)

War in Chang-An City

Chang-an in utter confusion
as though wolves and tigers had been
let loose; and I turned into a refugee
seeking to escape from my own country
to the borders of another; my home sad
and bitter that I must go; my friends wishing
to escape with me.

Leaving the city
one saw nothing, for the horror of the surroundings
blotted out all else; everywhere
the white bones of the dead were
scattered and on the roads were starving women
putting the children they could not feed
into the grass to die;
the abandoned child cries, yet the mother
dare not turn her head, though herself
shedding tears, saying she knew not where
she would die herself, and surely both
could not keep alive; and I, rather than
listen to such bitter words, goad my horse
along faster;
on the South I climb to Pa Ling, looking
back at Chang-an; then, thinking of the good king
who lies there, long with a broken heart
for the sweet day of peace.

(*Translated from the Chinese by Rewi Alley*)

MARGARET ROCKWELL (20th Century)

Hiroshima

A dream of waking in some sleeper's eye
Brought this broad estuary into time:
Here the blue limbs of seven rivers lie
Below mountains where no devils climb.
Clear-running waters, if your wink of birth
Focussed a flash where dark fatality
Mirrored an instant shrivelling the earth,
No thing remembered.
           Factuality
Built Mori's castle, and the central pond
Of Lord Asano's garden caught the light
Across the seasons; in the sea beyond
The sacred gateway shone, vermilion bright:
No thing revealed, no thing could whisper of
The moment that would force you into love.

One August morning, still and very clear,
Came the superfortress from the south,
Dragon with a lantern in his mouth
To light the way to hell: proud pioneer:
Red fig dropped slow and first, as if to feed
A thousand angels, burst to blue-white glow—
Then broke all fury's furnace, and below
Tombstones bleached and tottered and the seed
Fell down in mortal rain.
           By evening
Only the screams of children, and the hiss
And murmur of wild fire. . . . Was that the kiss
Of some compassionate grave god descending?
So to reveal in rage the whisper of
The moment that would force the world to love.

The Flower Market

In the Royal City spring is almost over:
Tinkle, tinkle—the coaches and the horsemen pass.
We tell each other "This is the peony season":
And follow with the crowd that goes to the Flower Market.
"Cheap and dear—no uniform price:
The cost of the plant depends on the number of blossoms.
For the fine flower,—a hundred pieces of damask:
For the cheap flower,—five bits of silk.
Above is spread an awning to protect them;
Around is woven a wattle fence to screen them.
When they are transplanted, they will not lose their beauty."
Each household thoughtlessly follows the custom,
Man by man, no one realizing.
There happened to be an old farm labourer
Who came by chance that way.
He bowed his head and sighed a deep sigh:
But this sigh nobody understood.
He was thinking, "A cluster of deep-red flowers
Would pay the taxes of ten poor houses."

A Ballad on the Taxes

Good people, what, will you of all be bereft—
Will you never learn wit while a penny is left?
You are all like the dog in the fable betray'd,
To let go the substance and snatch at the shade;
With specious pretences, and foreign expenses,
   We war for Religion, and waste all our chink,
'Tis nipped, and 'tis clipped, 'tis lent, and 'tis spent,
   Till 'tis gone, 'tis gone to the Devil I think.

We pay for our new-born, we pay for our dead,
We pay if we're single, we pay if we're wed;
To show that our merciful senate don't fail,
They begin at our head and tax down to the tail.
We pay through the nose by subjecting foes,
   Yet for all our expenses get nothing but blows;
At home we are cheated, abroad we're defeated,
   But the end on't, the end on't—the Lord above knows!

We parted with all our old money, to shew
We foolishly hope for a plenty of new;
But might have remember'd, when we came to the push,
That a bird in the hand is worth two in the bush:
We now like poor wretches are kept under hatches,
   At rack and at manger like beasts in the ark,
Since our burgesses and knights make us pay for our lights—
   Why should we, why should we be kept in the dark?

The War Year

Lowland hills and rivers
                dragged on to the war map
   O lowland lowlands O!
Those groaning people!
             how can they live?
                 A turnip or two
                 grubbed up
Don't talk to me
            about titles
            promotions
            all that slop
One general
         pulling out a victory
    leaves
              ten
              thousand
              corpses
                   to rot!

           (Translated from the Chinese by
       C. H. Kwock and Vincent McHugh)

Does It Matter?

Does it matter—losing your legs? . . .
For people will always be kind,
And you need not show that you mind
When the others come in after hunting
To gobble their muffins and eggs.

Does it matter—losing your sight? . . .
There's such splendid work for the blind;
And people will always be kind,
As you sit on the terrace remembering
And turning your face to the light.

Do they matter—those dreams from the pit? . . .
You can drink and forget and be glad,
And people won't say that you're mad;
For they'll know that you've fought for your country,
And no one will worry a bit.

WILLIAM LANGLAND (c. 1332–c. 1400)

Friars

Friars? All the four orders, I found them there,
Preaching to the people, and glosing the gospel
For their own profit.

Many of these masters may dress as they will,
Money and their preaching soon meet one another.
Gods love has turned trader, and the rich pay high,
And we in few years have seen wonderful things.
If Gods love and the Church do not cut down such Friars,
The greatest mischief in the world will mount up full fast.

Look there, a Pardoner, preaching like a priest,
A papal bull he brought, sealed by the bishop,
He can assoil them all, of fasting, falsehood, and of broken vows.

The simple fools believed him, loved his words,
Came and knelt and kissed his bull,
He bunched his "letters" in their faces and blinded their eyes,
And his parchment roll robbed them of rings and brooches.

Thus, men, ye give your gold to keep gluttons going,
And lend it to loafers that follow lechery.

. . .

But against the bishop your Pardoner preaches not,
For the parson and the Pardoner share the sermon-silver,
Which the parish poor would get if the Pardoner were away.

Some parish priests complained to the bishop,
The parish was poor since the Great Pestilence,
Praying for licence in London to dwell,
And sing masses for souls for silver is sweet.

(*from* PIERS PLOWMAN)

The Preacher and the Slave

(TUNE: *"Sweet Bye and Bye"*)

Long-haired preachers come out every night,
Try to tell you what's wrong and what's right;
But when asked how 'bout something to eat
They will answer with voices so sweet:

CHORUS:

You will eat, bye and bye,
In that glorious land above the sky;
Work and pray, live on hay,
You'll get pie in the sky when you die.

And the starvation army they play,
And they sing and they clap and they pray.
Till they get all your coin on the drum,
Then they tell you when you are on the bum:

If you fight hard for children and wife—
Try to get something good in this life—
You're a sinner and bad man, they tell,
When you die you will sure go to hell.

Workingmen of all countries unite,
Side by side we for freedom will fight:
When the world and its wealth we have gained
To the grafters we'll sing this refrain:

LAST CHORUS:

You will eat, bye and bye.
When you've learned how to cook and to fry;
Chop some wood, 'twill do you good,
And you'll eat in the sweet bye and bye.

The Lie

Go, Soul, the body's guest,
  Upon a thankless arrant:*
Fear not to touch the best;
  The truth shall be thy warrant:
Go, since I needs must die,
And give the world the lie.

Say to the court, it glows
  And shines like rotten wood;
Say to the church, it shows
  What's good, and doth no good:
If church and court reply,
Then give them both the lie.

Tell potentates, they live
  Acting by others' action;
Not loved unless they give,
  Not strong but by their faction:
If potentates reply,
Give potentates the lie.

Tell men of high condition,
  That manage the estate,
Their purpose is ambition,
  Their practice only hate:
And if they once reply,
Then give them all the lie.

Tell them that brave it most,
  They beg for more by spending,
Who in their greatest cost,
  Seek nothing but commending:
And if they make reply,
Then give them all the lie.

---

* errand

16

Tell zeal it wants devotion;
    Tell love it is but lust;
Tell time it is but motion;
    Tell flesh it is but dust:
And wish them not reply,
For thou must give the lie.

Tell age it daily wasteth;
    Tell honor how it alters;
Tell beauty how she blasteth;
    Tell favor how it falters:
And as they shall reply,
Give every one the lie.

Tell wit how much it wrangles
    In tickle points of niceness;
Tell wisdom she entangles
    Herself in over-wiseness:
And when they do reply,
Straight give them both the lie.

Tell physic of her boldness;
    Tell skill it is pretention;
Tell charity of coldness;
    Tell law it is contention:
And as they do reply,
So give them still the lie.

Tell fortune of her blindness;
    Tell nature of decay;
Tell friendship of unkindness;
    Tell justice of delay;
And if they will reply,
Then give them all the lie.

Tell arts they have no soundness,
    But vary by esteeming;
Tell schools they want profoundness,
    And stand too much on seeming:
If arts and schools reply,
Give arts and schools the lie.

Tell faith it's fled the city;
    Tell how the country erreth;

Tell, manhood shakes off pity;
    Tell, virtue least preferreth:
And if they do reply,
Spare not to give the lie.

So when thou hast, as I
    Commanded thee, done blabbing,—
Although to give the lie
    Deserves no less than stabbing,—
Stab at thee he that will,
No stab the soul can kill.

The Lion and O'Reilly

"Who'll rage against all government
That leaves the heart unheeded?"
"Who'll not?" cried out O'Reilly,
As he beat on the bar, unheeded.

"I've heard that said these fifty years
And still we're governmented,"
Murmured a man with dulling eyes,
But no one else assented.

"The heart's a thing won't let us down;
The head is too confusing.
Who thinks about his heart too much
Will find himself refusing."

"But the mind is strong when the heart is
And red blood fills the veins.
So up and rinse your minds, boys,
With life-blood till it pains."

"A fight was fought some years ago
For freedom from the Lion.
Why should we now be roared at by
Some tyrant named O'Ryan?"

"We'll make a way for freedom
By thinking of bigger things
Than officials with their inkpot skulls
And forms with long green strings."

"Who'll move this motion with me?
Who'll first and second it?"
"Who'll not?" cried out O'Reilly,
Splitting the board with a final hit.

WILLIAM SHAKESPEARE (1564–1616)

Upon the King

Upon the King! let us our lives, our souls,
Our debts, our careful wives,
Our children, and our sins lay on the King!
We must bear all. O hard condition,
Twin-born with greatness, subject to the breath
Of every fool, whose sense no more can feel
But his own wringing! What infinite heart's-ease
Must kings neglect, that private men enjoy!
And what have kings, that privates have not too,
Save ceremony, save general ceremony?
And what art thou, thou idol Ceremony?

. . . .

Canst thou, when thou command'st the beggar's knee,
Command the health of it? No, thou proud dream,
That play'st so subtly with a king's repose;
I am a king that find thee, and I know
'Tis not the balm, the sceptre: and the ball,
The sword, the mace, the crown imperial,
The intertissued robe of gold and pearl,
The farced title running 'fore the King,
The throne he sits on, nor the tide of pomp
That beats upon the high shore of this world,
No, not all these, thrice-gorgeous Ceremony,—
Not all these, laid in bed majestical,
Can sleep so soundly as the wretched slave,
Who with a body fill'd and vacant mind
Gets him to rest, cramm'd with distressful bread,
Never sees horrid night, the child of hell,

. . . .

And, but for ceremony, such a wretch
Winding up days with toil and nights with sleep,
Had the fore-hand and vantage of a king.
The slave, a member of the country's peace,
Enjoys it, but in gross brain little wots
What watch the King keeps to maintain the peace,
Whose hours the peasant best advantages.

(*from* HENRY V, ACT IV, *Scene i, lines 247–301*)

Abraham Lincoln Walks at Midnight

(in Springfield, Illinois)

It is portentous, and a thing of state
That here at midnight in our little town,
A mourning figure walks, and will not rest,
Near the old court-house pacing up and down.

Or by his homestead, or in shadowed yards,
He lingers where his children used to play;
Or through the market, on the well-worn stones,
He stalks until the dawn-stars burn away.

A bronzed lank man! His suit of ancient black,
A famous high top-hat and plain worn shawl,
Make him the quaint great figure that men love,
The prairie lawyer, master of us all.

He cannot sleep upon his hillside now.
He is among us—as in times before!
And we who toss and lie awake for long
Breathe deep, and start, to see him pass the door.

His head is bowed. He thinks on men and kings.
Yea, when the sick world cries, how can he sleep?
Too many peasants fight, they know not why;
Too many homesteads in black terror weep.

The sins of all the war-lords burn his heart.
He sees the dreadnaughts scouring every main.
He carries on his shawl-wrapped shoulders now
The bitterness, the folly and the pain.

He cannot rest until a spirit-dawn
Shall come—the shining hope of Europe free:
The league of sober folk, the Workers' Earth,
Bringing long peace to Cornland, Alp and Sea.

It breaks his heart that kings must murder still,
That all his hours of travail here for men
Seem yet in vain. And who will bring white peace
That he may sleep upon his hill again?

WILLIAM SHAKESPEARE (1564–1616)

Poor Naked Wretches

In, boy; go first. You houseless poverty,—
Nay, get thee in. I'll pray, and then I'll sleep.
    (*Exit Fool*)
Poor naked wretches, wheresoe'er you are,
That bide the pelting of this pitiless storm,
How shall your houseless heads and unfed sides,
Your loop'd and window'd raggedness, defend you
From seasons such as these? O, I have ta'en
Too little care of this! Take physic, pomp;
Expose thyself to feel what wretches feel,
That thou mayst shake the superflux to them,
And show the heavens more just.

  (*from* KING LEAR, *Act III, Scene iii, lines 26–36*)

Two Bums Walk Out of Eden

Two bums walk out of Eden. Evening approaches
The suave, the decorous trees, the careful grass,
The strict green benches—and the two bums go.

They caught the official nod, the backward-pointing
Thumb, and now they rise and leave a little
Briskly as men heedful to waste no time—

As men bending their steps toward due appointments.
The tall one looms like a skeleton; the runt
Walks with the totter of a tumbleweed.

Down the trimmed ceremonial path they go
Together, silent and separate and eyes
Ahead like soldiers. Down the long path and out.

What desert blanched these faces? What blowing sands
Gullied the eyes and wrecked the hanging hands
While Babylon and Nineveh were falling?

Now a shade darker will be a shade less dark.
Now there is room for evening in the park
Where cool episcopal bells are calling, calling.

Death

Death, be not proud, though some have called thee
Mighty and dreadful, for thou art not so:
For those whom thou think'st thou dost overthrow
Die not, poor Death; nor yet canst thou kill me.
From Rest and Sleep, which but thy picture be,
Much pleasure, then from thee much more must flow;
And soonest our best men with thee do go—
Rest of their bones and souls' delivery!
Thou'rt slave to fate, chance, kings, and desperate men,
And dost with poison, war, and sickness dwell;
And poppy or charms can make us sleep as well
And better than thy stroke. Why swell'st thou then?
   One short sleep past, we wake eternally,
    And Death shall be no more: Death, thou shalt die!

Do Not Go Gentle into That Good Night

Do not go gentle into that good night,
Old age should burn and rave at close of day;
Rage, rage against the dying of the light.

Though wise men at their end know dark is right,
Because their words had forked no lightning they
Do not go gentle into that good night.

Good men, the last wave by, crying how bright
Their frail deeds might have danced in a green bay,
Rage, rage against the dying of the light.

Wild men who caught and sang the sun in flight,
And learn, too late, they grieved it on its way,
Do not go gentle into that good night.

Grave men, near death, who see with blinding sight
Blind eyes could blaze like meteors and be gay,
Rage, rage against the dying of the light.

And you, my father, there on the sad height,
Curse, bless, me now with your fierce tears, I pray.
Do not go gentle into that good night.
Rage, rage against the dying of the light.

Song

Go and catch a falling star,
   Get with child a mandrake root,
Tell me where all past years are,
   Or who cleft the Devil's foot;
Teach me to hear mermaids singing,
Or to keep off envy's stinging,
       And find
       What wind
Serves to advance an honest mind.

If thou be'st born to strange sights,
   Things invisible to see,
Bide ten thousand days and nights
   Till Age snow white hairs on thee;
Thou, when thou return'st wilt tell me
All strange wonders that befell thee,
       And swear
       No where
Lives a woman true and fair.

If thou findest one, let me know;
   Such pilgrimage were sweet.
Yet do not; I would not go,
   Though at next door we might meet.
Though she were true when you met her,
And last till you write your letter,
       Yet she
       Will be
False, ere I come, to two or three.

To The Ladies

Moves in me now the tongues, the gongs
Of women in unreason: gold cats so purred
With pride, twitching, and blinking murd-
Er from broom's corner; belles with dragged songs
Of pity in the voicing, tolling out
Woes and whys and when and if and but.
Such claws, such cause, such caterwauling noise:
Alas, that girls should ever marry boys!

Could Adam, when the raging rib was taken
Have prevented it, that round and milky form
Among the trees, surer than God and warm
With power, watching until the tree is shaken,
Hearing her sister come, waiting the hiss
To turn her to a Mrs. from a Miss . . . ?

The Vanity of the World

False world, thou ly'st: thou canst not lend
       The least delight:
Thy favors cannot gain a friend,
       They are so slight:
Thy morning pleasures make an end
       To please at night:
Poor are the wants that thou supply'st,
And yet thou vaunt'st, and yet thou vy'st
With heaven; fond earth, thou boast'st; false world, thou ly'st.

Thy babbling tongue tells golden tales
       Of endless treasure;
Thy bounty offers easy sales
       Of lasting pleasure;
Thou ask'st the conscience what she ails,
       And swear'st to ease her:
There's none can want where thou supply'st:
There's none can give when thou deny'st.
Alas! fond world, thou boast'st; false world thou ly'st.

What well advised ear regards
       What earth can say?
Thy words are gold, but thy rewards
       Are painted clay:
Thy cunning can but pack the cards,
       Thou canst not play:
Thy game at weakest, still thou vy'st;
If seen, and then revy'd, deny'st:
Thou art not what thou seem'st; false world, thou ly'st.

   •   •   •   •   •   •   •

What mean dull souls, in this high measure,
       To haberdash
In earth's base wares, whose greatest treasure
       Is dross and trash?
The height of whose enchanting pleasure
       Is but a flash?

Are these the goods that thou supply'st
Us mortals with? Are these the high'st?
Can these bring cordial peace? false world, thou ly'st.

(Abridged)

W. R. RODGERS (1911–   )

White Christmas

Punctually at Christmas the soft plush
Of sentiment snows down, embosoms all
The sharp and pointed shapes of venom, shawls
The hills and hides the shocking holes of this
Uneven world of want and wealth, cushions
With cosy wish like cotton-wool the cool
Arm's-length interstices of caste and class,
And into obese folds subtracts from sight
All truculent acts, bleeding the world white.

Punctually that glib pair, Peace and Goodwill,
Emerges royally to take the air,
Collect the bows, assimilate the smiles,
Of waiting men. It is a genial time;
Angels, like stalactites, descend from heaven;
Bishops distribute their own weight in words,
Congratulate the poor on Christlike lack;
And the member for the constituency
Feeds the five thousand, and has plenty back.

Punctually, to-night, in old stone circles
Of set reunion, families stiffly sit
And listen: this is the night and this the happy time
When the tinned milk of human kindness is
Upheld and holed by radio-appeal:
Hushed are hurrying heels on hard roads,
And every parlour's a pink pond of light
To the cold and travelling man going by
In the dark, without a bark or a bite.

But punctually to-morrow you will see
All this silent and dissembling world

Of stilted sentiment suddenly melt
Into mush and watery welter of words
Beneath the warm and moving traffic of
Feet and actual fact. Over the stark plain
The silted mill-chimneys once again spread
Their sackcloth and ashes, a flowing mane
Of repentance for the false day that's fled.

JAMES SHIRLEY (1596–1666)

Death the Leveler

The glories of our blood and state
　　Are shadows, not substantial things;
There is no armor against Fate;
　　Death lays his icy hand on kings:
　　　　Sceptre and Crown
　　　　Must tumble down,
And in the dust be equal made
With the poor crooked scythe and spade.

Some men with swords may reap the field,
　　And plant fresh laurels where they kill:
But their strong nerves at last must yield;
　　They tame but one another still:
　　　　Early or late
　　　　They stoop to fate,
And must give up their murmuring breath
When they, pale captives, creep to death.

The garlands wither on your brow;
　　Then boast no more your mighty deeds!
Upon Death's purple altar now
　　See where the victor-victim bleeds.
　　　　Your heads must come
　　　　To the cold tomb:
Only the actions of the just
Smell sweet and blossom in their dust.

Bells for John Whiteside's Daughter

There was such speed in her little body,
And such lightness in her footfall,
It is no wonder her brown study
Astonishes us all.

Her wars were bruited in our high window.
We looked among orchard trees and beyond,
Where she took arms against her shadow,
Or harried unto the pond

The lazy geese, like a snow cloud
Dripping their snow on the green grass,
Tricking and stopping, sleepy and proud,
Who cried in goose, Alas,

For the tireless heart within the little
Lady with rod that made them rise
From their noon apple-dreams and scuttle
Goose-fashion under the skies!

But now go the bells, and we are ready,
In one house we are sternly stopped
To say we are vexed at her brown study,
Lying so primly propped.

Metrum V

Happy that first white age when we
Lived by the Earth's mere charity!
No soft luxurious diet then
Had effeminated men:
No other meat, nor wine had any
Than the coarse mast, or simple honey;
And by the parents' care laid up,
Cheap berries did the children sup.
No pompous wear was in those days,
Of gummy silks or scarlet baize.
Their beds were on some flow'ry brink,
And clear spring-water was their drink.
The shady pine in the sun's heat
Was their cool and known retreat,
For then 'twas not cut down, but stood
The youth and glory of the wood.
The daring sailor with his slaves
Then had not cut the swelling waves,
Nor for desire of foreign store
Seen any but his native shore.
No stirring drum scarred that age,
Nor the shrill trumpets active rage,
No wounds by bitter hatred made
With warm blood soiled the shining blade;
For how could hostile madness arm
An age of love to public harm,
When common justice none withstood,
Nor sought rewards for spilling blood?
  O that at length our age would raise
Into the temper of those days!
But—worse than Etna's fires!—debate
And avarice inflame our State.
Alas! who was it that first found
Gold, hid of purpose under ground,
That sought out pearls, and dived to find
Such precious perils for mankind!

W. H. AUDEN (1907-   )

The Unknown Citizen

(To JS/07/M/378 This Marble Monument is Erected by the State)

He was found by the Bureau of Statistics to be
One against whom there was no official complaint,
And all the reports on his conduct agree
That, in the modern sense of an old-fashioned word, he was a
　　saint,
For in everything he did he served the Greater Community.
Except for the War till the day he retired
He worked in a factory and never got fired,
But satisfied his employers, Funge Motors Inc.
Yet he wasn't a scab or odd in his views,
For his Union reports that he paid his dues,
(Our report on his Union shows it was sound)
And our social Psychology workers found
That he was popular with his mates and liked a drink.
The Press are convinced that he bought a paper every day
And that his reactions to advertisements were normal in every
　　way.
Policies taken out in his name prove that he was fully insured,
And his Health-card shows he was once in hospital but left it
　　cured.
Both Producers Research and High-Grade Living declare
He was fully sensible to the advantage of the Installment Plan
And had everything necessary to the Modern Man,
A phonograph, a radio, a car and a frigidaire.
Our researchers into Public Opinion are content
That he held the proper opinions for the time of year;
When there was peace, he was for peace; when there was war,
　　he went.
He was married and added five children to the population,
Which our Eugenist says was the right number for a parent of
　　his generation,
And our teachers report that he never interfered with their
　　education.
Was he free? Was he happy? The question is absurd:
Had anything been wrong, we should certainly have heard.

Corinna, Pride of Drury-Lane

Corinna, pride of Drury-Lane,
For whom no shepherd sighs in vain;
Never did Covent-Garden boast
So bright a battered, strolling toast;
No drunken rake to pick her up,
No cellar where on tick to sup;
Returning at the midnight hour,
Four stories climbing to her bower;
Then, seated on a three-legged chair,
Takes off her artificial hair;
Now picking out a crystal eye,
She wipes it clean, and lays it by.
Her eyebrows from a mouse's hide
Stuck on with art on either side,
Pulls off with care, and first displays 'em,
Then in a play-book smoothly lays 'em.
Now dext'rously her plumpers draws,
That serve to fill her hollow jaws,
Untwists a wire, and from her gums
A set of teeth completely comes;
Pulls out the rags contrived to prop
Her flabby dugs, and down they drop.
Proceeding on, the lovely goddess
Unlaces next her steel-ribbed bodice,
Which, by the operator's skill,
Press down the lumps, the hollows fill.
Up goes her hand, and off she slips
The bolsters that supply her hips:
With gentlest touch she next explores
Her chancres, issues, running sores;
Effects of many a sad disaster,
And then to each applies a plaster:
But must, before she goes to bed,
Rub off the daubs of white and red.

(*from* A BEAUTIFUL NYMPH GOING TO BED)

Made in Heaven

From Heals and Harrods come her lovely bridegrooms
(One cheque alone furnished two bedrooms),

From a pantechnicon in the dog-paraded street
Under the orange plane leaves, on workmen's feet

Crunching over Autumn, the fruits of marriage brought
Craftsmen-felt wood, Swedish dresses a court

Stool tastefully imitated and the wide bed—
(the girl who married money kept her maiden head).

As things were ticked off the Harrods list, there grew
A middle-class maze to pick your way through—

The labour-saving kitchen to match the labour-saving thing
She'd fitted before marriage (O Love, with this ring

I thee wed)—lastly the stereophonic radiogram
And her Aunt's sly letter promising a pram.

Settled in now, the Italian honeymoon over,
As the relatives said, she was living in clover.

The discontented drinking of a few weeks stopped,
She awoke up one morning to her husband's alarm-clock,

Saw the shining faces of the wedding gifts from the bed,
Foresaw the cosy routine of the massive years ahead.

As she watched her husband knot his tie for the city,
She thought: I wanted to be a dancer once—it's a pity

I've done none of the things I thought I wanted to,
Found nothing more exacting than my own looks, get through

Half a dozen lovers whose faces I can't quite remember
(I can still start the Rose Adagio, one foot on the fender)

But at least I'm safe from everything but cancer—
The apotheosis of the young wife and mediocre dancer.

FABLE V

The Wild Boar and the Ram

Against an elm a sheep was tied,
The butcher's knife in blood was dyed;
The patient flock, in silent fright,
From far beheld the horrid sight;
A savage boar, who near them stood,
Thus mocked to scorn the fleecy brood.
    "All cowards should be served like you.
See, see, your murd'rer is in view;
With purple hands and reeking knife
He strips the skin yet warm with life:
Your quartered sires, your bleeding dams,
The dying bleat of harmless lambs
Call for revenge. O stupid race!
The heart that wants revenge is base."
    "I grant," an ancient ram replies,
"We bear no terror in our eyes,
Yet think us not of soul so tame,
Which no repeated wrongs inflame,
Insensible of ev'ry ill,
Because we want thy tusks to kill.
Know, those who violence pursue
Give to themselves the vengeance due,
For in these massacres they find
The two chief plagues that waste mankind.
Our skin supplies the wrangling bar,
It wakes their slumb'ring sons to war,
And well revenge may rest contented,
Since drums and parchment were invented."

What Were They Like?

(QUESTIONS AND ANSWERS)

1) Did the people of Viet Nam
    use lanterns of stone?
2) Did they hold ceremonies
    to reverence the opening of buds?
3) Were they inclined to rippling laughter?
4) Did they use bone and ivory,
    jade and silver, for ornament?
5) Had they an epic poem?
6) Did they distinguish between speech and singing?

1) Sir, their light hearts turned to stone.
    It is not remembered whether in gardens
    stone lanterns illumined pleasant ways.
2) Perhaps they gathered once to delight in blossom,
    but after the children were killed
    there were no more buds.
3) Sir, laughter is bitter to the burned mouth.
4) A dream ago, perhaps. Ornament is for joy.
    All the bones were charred.
5) It is not remembered. Remember,
    most were peasants; their life
    was in rice and bamboo.
    When peaceful clouds were reflected in the paddies
    and the water-buffalo stepped surely along terraces,
    maybe fathers told their sons old tales.
    When bombs smashed the mirrors
    there was time only to scream.
6) There is an echo yet, it is said,
    of their speech which was like a song.
    It is reported their singing resembled
    the flight of moths in moonlight.
    Who can say? It is silent now.

JOHN SCOTT OF AMWELL (1730–83)

Retort on the Foregoing

I hate that drum's discordant sound,
Parading round, and round, and round:
To thoughtless youth it pleasure yields,
And lures from cities and from fields,
To sell their liberty for charms
Of tawdry lace, and glittering arms;
And when Ambition's voice commands,
To march, and fight, and fall, in foreign lands.

I hate that drum's discordant sound,
Parading round, and round, and round:
To me it talks of ravag'd plains,
And burning towns, and ruin'd swains,
And mangled limbs, and dying groans,
And widows' tears, and orphans' moans;
And all that Misery's hand bestows,
To fill the catalogue of human woes.

THICH NHAT HANH (Contemporary Vietnamese)

Condemnation

Listen to this:
Yesterday six Vietcong came through my village.
Because of this my village was bombed—completely
    destroyed.
Every soul was killed.
When I come back to my village now, the day after,
There is nothing to see but clouds of dust and the river, still
    flowing.
The pagoda has neither roof nor altar.
Only the foundations of houses are left.
The bamboo thickets are burned away.

Here in the presence of the undisturbed stars,
In the invisible presence of all the people still alive on earth,
Let me raise my voice to denounce this filthy way,
This murder of brothers by brothers!
I have a question: Who pushed us into this killing of one
    another?

Whoever is listening, be my witness!
I cannot accept this war,
I never could, I never shall.
I have to say this a thousand times before I am killed.

I feel I am like a bird which dies for the sake of its mate,
Dripping blood from its broken beak, and crying out:
Beware! Turn around and face your real enemies—
Ambition, violence, hatred, greed.

Men cannot be our enemies—even men called "Vietcong"!
If we kill men, what brothers will we have left?
With whom shall we live then?

Sweet, Smiling Village

Sweet smiling village, loveliest of the lawn,
Thy sports are fled, and all thy charms withdrawn;
Amidst thy bowers the tyrant's hand is seen,
And desolation saddens all thy green;
One only master grasps the whole domain,
And half a tillage stints thy smiling plain.
No more thy glassy brook reflects the day,
But, choked with sedges, works its weedy way;
Along thy glades, a solitary guest,
The hollow-sounding bittern guards its nest;
Amidst thy desert walks the lapwing flies,
And tires their echoes with unvaried cries;
Sunk are thy bowers in shapeless ruin all,
And the long grass o'ertops the moldering wall;
And, trembling, shrinking from the spoiler's hand,
Far, far away thy children leave the land.

Ill fares the land, to hastening ills a prey,
Where wealth accumulates, and men decay.
Princes and lords may flourish, or may fade;
A breath can make them, as a breath has made;
But a bold peasantry, their country's pride,
When once destroyed, can never be supplied.

(*from* THE DESERTED VILLAGE)

The War Against the Trees

The man who sold his lawn to standard oil
Joked with his neighbors come to watch the show
While the bulldozers, drunk with gasoline,
Tested the virtue of the soil
Under the branchy sky
By overthrowing first the privet-row.

Forsythia-forays and hydrangea-raids
Were but preliminaries to a war
Against the great-grandfathers of the town,
So freshly lopped and maimed.
They struck and struck again,
And with each elm a century went down.

All day the hireling engines charged the trees,
Subverting them by hacking underground
In grub-dominions, where dark summer's mole
Rampages through his halls,
Till a northern seizure shook
Those crowns, forcing the giants to their knees.

I saw the ghosts of children at their games
Racing beyond their childhood in the shade,
And while the green world turned its death-foxed page
And a red wagon wheeled,
I watched them disappear
Into the suburbs of their grievous age.

Ripped from the craters much too big for hearts
The club-roots bared their amputated coils,
Raw gorgons matted blind, whose pocks and scars
Cried Moon! on a corner lot
One witness-moment, caught
In the rear-view mirrors of the passing cars.

TIMOTHY DWIGHT (1752–1817)

The Smooth Divine

There smiled the smooth Divine, unused to wound
The sinner's heart with hell's alarming sound.
No terrors on his gentle tongue attend;
No grating truths the nicest ear offend.
That strange new-birth, that methodistic grace,
Nor in his heart nor sermons found a place.
Plato's fine tales he clumsily retold,
Trite, fireside, moral seesaws, dull as old,—
His Christ and Bible placed at good remove,
Guilt hell-deserving, and forgiving love.
'Twas best, he said, mankind should cease to sin:
Good fame required it; so did peace within.
Their honors, well he knew, would ne'er be driven;
But hoped they still would please to go to heaven.
Each week he paid his visitation dues;
Coaxed, jested, laughed; rehearsed the private news;
Smoked with each goody, thought her cheese excelled;
Her pipe he lighted, and her baby held.
Or placed in some great town, with lacquered shoes,
Trim wig, and trimmer gown, and glistening hose,
He bowed, talked politics, learned manners mild,
Most meekly questioned, and most smoothly smiled;
At rich men's jests laughed loud, their stories praised,
Their wives' new patterns gazed, and gazed, and gazed;
Most daintily on pampered turkeys dined,
Nor shrunk with fasting, nor with study pined:
Yet from their churches saw his brethren driven,
Who thundered truth, and spoke the voice of heaven,
Chilled trembling guilt in Satan's headlong path,
Charmed the feet back, and roused the ear of death.
"Let fools," he cried, "starve on, while prudent I
Snug in my nest shall live, and snug shall die."

Thoughts on the Christian Doctrine of Eternal Hell

Is it not interesting to see
How the Christians continually
Try to separate themselves in vain
From the doctrine of eternal pain?

They cannot do it,
They are vowed to it,
The Lord said it,
They must believe it.

So the vulnerable body is stretched
  without pity
On flames forever. Is this not pretty?

The religion of Christianity
Is mixed of sweetness and cruelty.
Reject this Sweetness for she wears
A smoky dress out of hell fires.

Who makes a god, who paints him thus?
It is the Christian religion does.

Oh oh have none of it,
Blow it away, have done with it.

Americans!

Left to himself, wherever man is found,
In peace he aims to walk life's little round;
In peace to sail, in peace to till the soil,
Nor force false grandeur from a brother's toil.
All but the base, designing, scheming few,
Who seize on nations with a robber's view,
With crowns and sceptres awe his dazzled eye,
And priests that hold the artillery of the sky;
These, these, with armies, navies, potent grown,
Impoverish man and bid the nations groan.
These with pretended balances of states
Keep worlds at variance, breed eternal hates,
Make man the poor base slave of low design,
Degrade his nature to its last decline,
Shed hell's worse blots on his exalted race,
And make them poor and mean, to make them base.

Shall views like these assail our happy land,
Where embryo monarchs thirst for wide command,
Shall a whole nation's strength and fair renown
Be sacrific'd, to prop a tottering throne,
That, ages past, the world's great curse has stood,
Has throve on plunder, and been fed on blood?—
Americans! will you control such views?
Speak—for you must—you have no hour to lose.

(*from* REFLECTIONS)

45

American Primitive

Look at him there in his stovepipe hat,
His high-top shoes, and his handsome collar;
Only my Daddy could look like that,
And I love my Daddy like he loves his Dollar.

The screen door bangs, and it sounds so funny,
There he is in a shower of gold;
His pockets are stuffed with folding money,
His lips are blue, and his hands feel cold.

He hangs in the hall by his black cravat,
The ladies faint, and the children holler:
Only my Daddy could look like that,
And I love my Daddy like he loves his Dollar.

GEORGE CRABBE (1754-1832)

The Newspaper

I sing of NEWS, and all those vapid sheets
The rattling hawker vends through gaping streets;
Whate'er their name, whate'er the time they fly,
Damp from the press, to charm the reader's eye:
For soon as Morning dawns with roseate hue,
The HERALD of the morn arises too;
POST after POST succeeds, and, all day long,
GAZETTES and LEDGERS swarm, a noisy throng.
When evening comes, she comes with all her train
Of LEDGERS, CHRONICLES, and POSTS again.
Like bats, appearing when the sun goes down,
From holes obscure and corners of the town.
Of all these triflers, all like these, I write;
Oh! like my subject could my song delight,

. . .

These are the ills the teeming Press supplies,
The pois'nous springs from learning's fountain rise;
Not there the wise alone their entrance find,
Imparting useful light to mortals blind;
But, blind themselves, these erring guides hold out
Alluring lights to lead us far about;
Screen'd by such means, here Scandal whets her quill,
Here Slander shoots unseen, whene'er she will;
Here Fraud and Falsehood labour to deceive,
And Folly aids them both, impatient to believe.
Such, sons of Britain! are the guides ye trust;
So wise their counsel, their reports so just!—

(*from* THE NEWSPAPER)

ROBERT PETERSON (1924–)

Dear America

> "We are humanitarians." LYNDON B. JOHNSON
> "No lie lives forever." CARLYLE

Dear America you worry me.
Our friendship (& that's all it ever was)
is shaky.

I don't trust you
or your Dreams
or your Destiny
any more.

No longer Gem of the Ocean,
no longer Land of the Free,
your house no more the Golden Door

Who are you to ask me to be a statistic
or a lizard? (No I won't shut up.)

Trying to hand my body over to Ministers
& Generals, throwing me out False Reports,

killing kids & calling it News.

I know an ugly mirage when I see one.
Your Power grunts in cannon, is dying
in smoke rings . . .

Don't tell me what is good for me,
I'll make up my own poor mind.
The Last Mile is a lonesome road,
go bomb a canoe.

London

I wander through each charter'd street,
Near where the charter'd Thames does flow,
And mark in every face I meet
Marks of weakness, marks of woe.

In every cry of every Man,
In every Infant's cry of fear,
In every voice, in every ban
The mind-forg'd manacles I hear.

How the chimney-sweeper's cry
Every black'ning church appals;
And the hapless soldier's sigh
Runs in blood down palace walls.

But most through midnight streets I hear
How the youthful harlot's curse
Blasts the new-born infant's tear,
And blights with plagues the marriage hearse.

An Elementary School Class Room in a Slum

Far, far from gusty waves, these children's faces.
Like rootless weeds the torn hair round their paleness.
The tall girl with her weighed-down head. The paper-
seeming boy with rat's eyes. The stunted unlucky heir
Of twisted bones, reciting a father's gnarled disease,
His lesson from his desk. At back of the dim class,
One unnoted, sweet and young: his eyes live in a dream
Of squirrels' game, in tree room, other than this.

On sour cream walls, donations. Shakespeare's head
Cloudless at dawn, civilized dome riding all cities.
Belled, flowery, Tyrolese valley. Open-handed map
Awarding the world its world. And yet, for these
Children, these windows, not this world, are world,
Where all their future's painted with a fog,
A narrow street sealed in with a lead sky,
Far, far from rivers, capes, and stars of words.

Surely Shakespeare is wicked, the map a bad example
With ships and sun and love tempting them to steal—
For lives that slyly turn in their cramped holes
From fog to endless night? On their slag heap, these children
Wear skins peeped through by bones and spectacles of steel
With mended glass, like bottle bits on stones.
All of their time and space are foggy slum
So blot their maps with slums as big as doom.

Unless, governor, teacher, inspector, visitor,
This map becomes their window and these windows
That open on their lives like crouching tombs
Break, O break open, till they break the town
And show the children to the fields and all their world
Azure on their sands, to let their tongues
Run naked into books, the white and green leaves open
The history theirs whose language is the sun.

SAMUEL WESLEY (1766–1837)

On the Setting Up of Mr. Butler's Monument in Westminster Abbey

While Butler, needy wretch, was yet alive,
No generous patron would a dinner give:
See him, when starved to death and turned to dust,
Presented with a monumental bust!
The poet's fate is here in emblem shown:
He asked for bread, and he received a stone.

Asylum

"I said, 'You're right!' At last they've found
The perfect place for Ezra Pound.
I wish they'd put him there long since!
And yet I don't hate what he prints.
But now each form of mental ill
Must seek its house behind the hill;
And why should poetics alone
Bul-bul for the sane man's stone?

Let all who can't be normal come!
With Ezra raise our hated home.
Queerness be our quarantine
From the pledged plague of seeming sane.
There, knowing no rule but the ear,
We in our sound-proof cells will hear—
Whatever drums our eardrums beat—
Poetry, insanely sweet."

WILLIAM WORDSWORTH (1770-1850)

The World

The world is too much with us; late and soon,
  Getting and spending, we lay waste our powers;
  Little we see in Nature that is ours;
We have given our hearts away, a sordid boon!
This sea that bares her bosom to the moon;
  The winds that will be howling at all hours,
  And are up-gathered now like sleeping flowers;
For this, for everything, we are out of tune;
It moves us not.—Great God! I'd rather be
  A Pagan suckled in a creed outworn;
So might I, standing on this pleasant lea,
  Have glimpses that would make me less forlorn;
Have sight of Proteus rising from the sea;
  Or hear old Triton blow his wreathèd horn.

How They Came From the Blue Snows

How they came from the blue snows year after year
Into the stranger's arbor, under the rain;
Hearing the sandhill cranes at night, marching again
To the next continent with the great spear
Of starlight flying before them as they go
Into the africas, americas, exploring
Laughter, and an oracle always on the winds.

Now do we track the tiger in the mind.
Now do the swift deer leap the nerve and bone;
It snows in the heart. We penetrate
A dry and sunless continent of stone;
And the flight of birds from the summer hollow
We do not understand, we do not follow.

WILLIAM WORDSWORTH (1770–1850)

England, 1802 (i)

O Friend! I know not which way I must look
  For comfort, being, as I am, opprest,
  To think that now our life is only drest
For show; mean handy-work of craftsman, cook,
Or groom!—We must run glittering like a brook
  In the open sunshine, or we are unblest:
  The wealthiest man among us is the best:
No grandeur now in nature or in book
Delights us. Rapine, avarice, expense,
  This is idolatry; and these we adore:
  Plain living and high thinking are no more:
  The homely beauty of the good old cause
Is gone; our peace, our fearful innocence,
  And pure religion breathing household laws.

For the Lost Generation

Oddities composed the sum of the news.
$E = mc^2$
Was another weird
Evidence of the existence of Jews.

And Paris! All afternoon in someone's attic
We raised our glasses
And drank to the asses
Who ran the world and turned neurotic.

Ours was a wonderful party.
Everyone threw rice,
The fattest girls were nice,
The world was rich in wisecracks and confetti.

The war was a first wife, somebody's blunder,
Who was right, who lost,
Held nobody's interest,
The dog on top was as bad as the dog under.

Sometimes after whisky, at the break of day,
There was a weary look, trace
Of a tear on a face.
Face of the blue nights that were winging away.

Look back on it all, the faraway cost—
Crash and sweet blues
(O Hiroshima, O Jews)—
No generation was so gay as the lost.

PERCY BYSSHE SHELLEY (1792–1822)

War Is the Statesman's Game

War is the statesman's game, the priest's delight,
The lawyer's jest, the hired assassin's trade,
And, to those royal murderers, whose mean thrones
Are bought by crimes of treachery and gore,
The bread they eat, the staff on which they lean.
Guards, garbed in blood-red livery, surround
Their palaces, participate the crimes
That force defends, and from a nation's rage
Secure the crown, which all the curses reach
That famine, frenzy, woe and penury breathe.
These are the hired bravos who defend
The tyrant's throne—the bullies of his fear:
These are the sinks and channels of worst vice,
The refuse of society, the dregs
Of all that is most vile: their cold hearts blend.
Deceit with sternness, ignorance with pride,
All that is mean and villanous, with rage
Which hopelessness of good, and self-contempt,
Alone might kindle; they are decked in wealth,
Honour and power, then are sent abroad
To do their work. The pestilence that stalks
In gloomy triumph through some Eastern land
Is less destroying. They cajole with gold,
And promises of fame, the thoughtless youth
Already crushed with servitude: he knows
His wretchedness too late, and cherishes
Repentance for his ruin, when his doom
Is sealed in gold and blood!
Those too the tyrant serve, who skilled to snare
The feet of justice in the toils of law,
Stand, ready to oppress the weaker still;
And, right or wrong, will vindicate for gold,
Sneering at public virtue, which beneath
Their pitiless tread lies torn and trampled, where
Honour sits smiling at the sale of truth.

(from QUEEN MAB, *Book IV)*

Dulce et Decorum Est

Bent double, like old beggars under sacks,
Knock-kneed, coughing like hags, we cursed through sludge,
Till on the haunting flares we turned our backs,
And towards our distant rest began to trudge.
Men marched asleep. Many had lost their boots,
But limped on, blood-shod. All went lame, all blind;
Drunk with fatigue; deaf even to the hoots
Of gas-shells dropping softly behind.

Gas! Gas! Quick, boys!—An ecstasy of fumbling,
Fitting the clumsy helmets just in time,
But someone still was yelling out and stumbling
And floundering like a man in fire or lime.—
Dim through the misty panes and thick green light,
As under a green sea, I saw him drowning.
In all my dreams before my helpless sight
He plunges at me, guttering, choking, drowning.

If in some smothering dreams, you too could pace
Behind the wagon that we flung him in,
And watch the white eyes writhing in his face,
His hanging face, like a devil's sick of sin;
If you could hear, at every jolt, the blood
Come gargling from the froth-corrupted lungs,
Bitter as the cud
Of vile, incurable sores on innocent tongues,
My friend, you would not tell with such high zest
To children ardent for some desperate glory,
The old Lie: Dulce et decorum est
Pro patria mori.

The Song of the Shirt

With fingers weary and worn,
　With eyelids heavy and red,
A woman sat, in unwomanly rags,
　Plying her needle and thread—
Stitch! stitch! stitch!
　In poverty, hunger, and dirt,
And still with a voice of dolorous pitch
　She sang the "Song of the Shirt."

　　　　*　*　*

"Work—work—work,
　Till the brain begins to swim;
Work—work—work,
　Till the eyes are heavy and dim!
Seam, and gusset, and band,
　Band, and gusset, and seam,
Till over the buttons I fall asleep,
　And sew them on in a dream!

"Oh, men, with sisters dear!
　Oh, men, with mothers and wives!
It is not linen you're wearing out
　But human creatures' lives!
Stitch—stitch—stitch,
　In poverty, hunger, and dirt,
Sewing at once, with a double thread
　A Shroud as well as a Shirt.

"But why do I talk of Death?
　That phantom of grisly bone,
I hardly fear its terrible shape,
　It seems so like my own—
It seems so like by own,
　Because of the fasts I keep;

Oh, God! that bread should be so dear,
    And flesh and blood so cheap!

"Work—work—work!
    My labor never flags;
And what are its wages? A bed of straw,
    A crust of bread—and rags.
That shattered roof—this naked floor—
    A table—a broken chair—
And a wall so blank, my shadow I thank
    For sometimes falling there!

"Work—work—work!
    From weary chime to chime,
Work—work—work,
    As prisoners work for crime!
Band, and gusset, and seam,
    Seam, and gusset, and band,
Till the heart is sick, and the brain benumbed,
    As well as the weary hand.

. . .

Seam, and gusset, and band,
    Band, and gusset, and seam,
Work—work—work,
    Like the engine that works by steam!
A mere machine of iron and wood
    That toils for Mammon's sake,
Without a brain to ponder and craze
    Or a heart to feel—and break!

With fingers weary and worn,
    With eyelids heavy and red,
A woman sat, in unwomanly rags,
    Plying her needle and thread—
Stitch! stitch! stitch!
    In poverty, hunger, and dirt,
And still with a voice of dolorous pitch—
Would that its tone could reach the rich!—
    She sang this "Song of the Shirt!"

(*Abridged*)

SARAH N. CLEGHORN (1876–1959)

The Golf Links

The golf links lie so near the mill
 That almost every day
The laboring children can look out
 And see the men at play.

VACHEL LINDSAY (1879–1931)

The Leaden-Eyed

Let not young souls be smothered out before
They do quaint deeds and fully flaunt their pride.
It is the world's one crime its babes grow dull,
Its poor are ox-like, limp and leaden-eyed.
Not that they starve, but starve so dreamlessly;
Not that they sow, but that they seldom reap;
Not that they serve, but have no gods to serve;
Not that they die, but that they die like sheep.

Port Authority Terminal: 9 A.M. Monday

From buses beached like an invasion fleet
They fill the waiting room with striding feet.

Their faces, white, and void of hate or pity,
Move on tall bodies toward the conquered city.

Among the lesser breeds of black and brown
They board their taxis with an absent frown,

Each to his concrete citadel,
To rule the city and to buy and sell.

At five o'clock they ride the buses back,
Leaving their Irish to guard the brown and black.

At six a drink, at seven dinner's served.
At ten or twelve, depressed, undressed, unnerved,

They mount their wives, dismount, they doze and dream
Apocalyptic Negroes in a stream

Of moving torches, marching from the slums,
Beating a band of garbage pails for drums,

Marching, with school-age children in their arms,
Advancing on the suburbs and the farms,

To integrate the schools and burn the houses . . .
The normal morning comes, the clock arouses

Junior and senior executive alike.
Back on the bus, and down the usual pike.

From buses beached like an invasion fleet
They fill the waiting room with striding feet.

To Make the People Happy

To make the people happy, lash them with guns.
The great words are empty, the high-sounding ones,
Fraternity, Justice, the Mission of France,
Liberty, Progress, Human Rights, Tolerance;
Socrates was mad; read Lélut and learn;
Christ, demagogue with a socialist turn,
Is much over-rated; the cannon is God,
Paixhans is its prophet; Earth, throw up your sod!
Man's ultimate aim is to learn how to kill.
The sword is the way to keep the people still.
Man's greatest achievement: the bullet. His star,
The light of a Lancaster bomb from afar.
His highest admirations under the sun,
The Armstrong mortar and the Cavalli gun.
God was mistaken: Caesar transcends:
In the beginning the Word; with Caesar it ends.
To think is sedition; to speak—worst of all!
The voice is for silence, the mind is—to crawl;
The world's on its belly, and man's greatness of yore,
Turns flabby and trembles; and—Peace! says War.

Bombing Casualties: Spain

Doll's faces are rosier but these were children
their eyes not glass but gleaming gristle
dark lenses in whose quicksilvery glances
the sunlight quivered. These blanched lips
were warm once and bright with blood
but blood
held in a moist blob of flesh
not split and spatter'd in tousled hair.

In these shadowy tresses
red petals did not always
thus clot and blacken to a scar.

These are dead faces:
wasps' nests are not more wanly waxen
wood embers not so greyly ashen.

They are laid out in ranks
like paper lanterns that have fallen
after a night of riot
extinct in the dry morning air.

Ode

Inscribed to W. H. Channing

Though loath to grieve
The evil time's soul patriot,
I cannot leave
My honied thought
For the priest's cant,
Or statesman's rant.

If I refuse
My study for their politique,
Which at the best is trick,
The angry Muse
Puts confusion in my brain.

But who is he that prates
Of the culture of mankind,
Of better arts and life?
Go, blindworm, go,
Behold the famous States
Harrying Mexico
With rifle and with knife!

Or who, with accent bolder,
Dare praise the freedom-loving mountaineer?
I found by thee, O rushing Contoocook!
And in thy valleys, Agiochook!
The jackals of the negro-holder.

The God who made New Hampshire
Taunted the lofty land
With little men;—
Small bat and wren
House in the oak:—
If earth-fire cleave
The upheaved land, and bury the folk,
The southern crocodile would grieve.

Virtue palters; Right is hence;
Freedom praised, but hid;
Funeral eloquence
Rattles the coffin-lid.

What boots thy zeal,
O glowing friend,
That would indignant rend
The northland from the south?
Wherefore? to what good end?
Boston Bay and Bunker Hill
Would serve things still;—
Things are of the snake.

The horseman serves the horse,
The neathered serves the neat,
The merchant serves the purse,
The eater serves his meat;
'Tis the day of the chattel,
Web to weave, and corn to grind;
Things are in the saddle,
And ride mankind.

(Abridged)

The Plot to Assassinate the Chase Manhattan Bank

To assassinate the Chase Manhattan Bank
Is not as easy as you'd think.
I walked in, see, and yelled "Kings-X!"
and saw what looked like great machines
come rumbling to a halt, and I thought,
fine—I'm halfway home. Then God rose from
the Office of the President,
a little miffed, I think, and said,
"What's on your mind?"
"I came up from the Coast," I said,
"to blow this pad to—if you will
excuse my pun—to Kingdom Come."
"You can't do that, my Son," he said,
and that's how I knew he was God,
although he looked a great deal
like John Wayne. "You wouldn't want,"
he said, "to do away with this—"
and from each teller's cage, a flock
of rainbow doves flew up, and settled
near the roof. "Put down your bomb,
let's have a talk," he said, and smiled.
I laid aside the bomb and followed him
into his office, and sat down.
"The Proletariat demands," I said,
"You cease this madness"; And he
smiled again. I saw he had a golden tooth.
"Some for the glories of this world,"
God said, then showed a picture of his family,
and then his house, a nice split-level
place up in the Bronx. His wife,
a pleasant-looking woman,
had inscribed it: "Love, In God We Trust."
He wiped away the tears that gathered
in the corners of his steely eyes,
choked back a sob, and called The Fuzz.
Inside a minute, forty cops popped from
the walls and drawers, came running from

the vault where God kept love, and
clamped the irons around my feet.
"Now Jean Valjean," God shouted,
gaining his composure, "now you'll
face the rack!" I pleaded it was all
a joke. I said I'd be a good li'l boy
and stay home playing with my spiders
if he'd let me go. But his bit was not
forgiveness, and they locked me in
a dungeon full of nasty things he had
discarded, like the stars,
and sea-foam, and the earth.

The Jewish Cemetery at Newport

How strange it seems! These Hebrews in their graves,
　　Close by the street of this fair seaport town,
Silent beside the never-silent waves,
　　At rest in all this moving up and down!

The trees are white with dust, that o'er their sleep
　　Wave their broad curtains in the south wind's breath,
While underneath such leafy tents they keep
　　The long, mysterious Exodus of Death.

And these sepulchral stones, so old and brown,
　　That pave with level flags their burial-place,
Seem like the tablets of the Law, thrown down
　　And broken by Moses at the mountain's base.

The very names recorded here are strange,
　　Of foreign accent, and of different climes;
Alvares and Rivera interchange
　　With Abraham and Jacob of old times.

"Blessed by God! for He created Death!"
　　The mourners said, "and death is rest and peace";
Then added, in the certainty of faith,
　　"And giveth life that never more shall cease."

Closed are the portals of their Synagogue,
　　No Psalms of David now the silence break,
No Rabbi reads the ancient Decalogue
　　In the grand dialect the Prophets spake.

Gone are the living, but the dead remain,
　　And not neglected; for a hand unseen,
Scattering its bounty, like a summer rain,
　　Still keeps their graves and their remembrance green.

How came they here? What burst of Christian hate,
　　What persecution, merciless and blind,

Drove o'er the sea—that desert desolate—
    These Ishmaels and Hagars of mankind?

They lived in narrow streets and lanes obscure,
    Ghetto and Judenstrass, in mirk and mire;
Taught in the school of patience to endure
    The life of anguish and the death of fire.

All their lives long, with the unleavened bread
    And bitter herbs of exile and its fears.
The wasting famine of the heart they fed,
    And slaked its thirst with marah of their tears.

Anathema maranatha! was the cry
    That rang from town to town, from street to street:
At every gate the accursed Mordicai
    Was mocked and jeered, and spurned by Christian feet.

Pride and humiliation hand in hand
    Walked with them through the world where'er they went,
Trampled and beaten were they as the sand,
    And yet unshaken as the continent.

For in the background figures vague and vast
    Of patriarchs and of prophets rose sublime,
And all the great traditions of the Past
    They saw reflected in the coming time.

And thus forever with reverted look
    The mystic volume of the world they read,
Spelling it backward, like a Hebrew book,
    Till life became a legend of the Dead.

But ah! what once has been shall be no more!
    The groaning earth in travail and in pain
Brings forth its races, but does not restore,
    And the dead nations never rise again.

The Permanent Delegate

My name is Jew.
  I come from the land of skeleton.
They beat me in Berlin,
    tortured me in Warsaw,
      shot me in Lublin
And I am still here—the ash of my bones
  a glowing monument, a fiery headstone.

I am the scorched hair of a virgin's bright curls
  smoothed and patted by anxious hands
I am a maddened mother's futile tears
  soothing in vain a hundred anguished hurts.

I am the spasm of a body convulsed in flames,
  the crumbling of a skeleton,
the boiling of blood, shriveling of flesh,
  smouldering ash of six million—
ashes of body, of brain, of vision, of work
  ashes of genius and dreams,
      ashes of God's master stroke—Man

Count the limbs, gentlemen—
  match them if you can in pairs.
    It can't be done.
For I am one ghost of six million.
Out of all the ashes I have become one
And the dream lies broken and spit on.

I am here to tell you, gentlemen
  it's a lie—the world is not yet Hitler-free.
Millions see it, condemn it,
  cry out my pain and warn you.

But you are moved like a granite statue
    by the prick of a pin.
Therefore I have come,
    uninvited, unwelcome
      bringing a message
from the land of skeleton.

I am grafting my ash to your souls.
I am hanging my dreams around your necks.
I am blotting out the sun from your day
                with my shadow.
I am tearing the quiet of your night
                with the shrieks of my tortures.
I will beat at your conscience
    with the hands of a million dead children and
I will pick at your brains
              with my maggots.

Yea, though you split the atom to infinity
    you will see my face before your eyes.
I sit at all the round tables
At every conference I am a delegate,
my credentials signed by six million
    from the land of skeleton
and you will never get rid of me
    until the world is Hitler-free.

*(Translated from the Yiddish by Max Rosenfeld and
Walter Lowenfels)*

JOHN GREENLEAF WHITTIER (1807-92)

Clerical Oppressors

Just God! and these are they
Who minister at thine altar, God of Right!
Men who their hands with prayer and blessing lay
    On Israel's Ark of light!

What! preach and kidnap men?
Give thanks, and rob thy own afflicted poor?
Talk of thy glorious liberty, and then
    Bolt hard the captive's door?

What! servants of thy own
Merciful Son, who came to seek and save
The homeless and the outcast, fettering down
    The tasked and plundered slave!

Pilate and Herod, friends!
Chief priests and rulers, as of old, combine!
Just God and holy! is that church, which lends
    Strength to the spoiler, thine?

Paid hypocrites, who turn
Judgement aside, and rob the Holy Book
Of those high words of truth which search and burn
    In warning and rebuke;

Feed fat, ye locusts, feed!
And, in your tasseled pulpits, thank the Lord
That, from the toiling bondman's utter need,
    Ye pile your own full board.

How long, O Lord! how long
Shall such a priesthood barter truth away,
And in Thy name, for robbery and wrong
    At Thy own altars pray?

Is not Thy hand stretched forth
Visibly in the heavens, to awe and smite?
Shall not the living God of all the earth,
    And heaven above, do right?

Woe, then, to all who grind
Their brethren of a common Father down!
To all who plunder from the immortal mind
    Its bright and glorious crown!

Woe to the priesthood! woe
To those whose hire is with the price of blood;
Perverting, darkening, changing, as they go,
    The searching truths of God!

Their glory and their might
Shall perish; and their very names shall be
Vile before all the people, in the light
    Of a world's liberty.

Oh, speed the moment on
When Wrong shall cease, and Liberty and Love
And Truth and Right throughout the earth be known
    As in their home above.

They Got You Last Night

. . . They got you last night.
I saw you clubbed.
I recognized the nightsticks: they were thorny twigs

From the tree from where I saw
your brother lynched.
They felt the same as those they used
on my Father in Maidenek.

I saw a boot step on your throat last night:
it was the same boot that stepped on my young sister's throat.

I saw you shot last night.
I saw the gun: it was the gun they used
on my brother in Dachau . . .

I saw clear white, pure white
from White House to the Ku Klux Klan's white robes
and the white gardenias in the lapels of justice—
white guns booming in Mississippi courthouses.
white guns on campuses proclaiming
white law of love and brotherhood . . .

I saw Christ flog you on the chain gang.
I saw Christ put the torch to your brother on a heartbroken
    tree.
I saw Christ torture you on Times Square.
(That wasn't Christ at all, of course—it was Judas raving he
    was Christ, with thumb on trigger).
I saw your children chased from a white open hydrant on a
    hot day in Alexandria. I wanted to cry,
but would not dare
after I heard your mothers crying from a million
smoke holes in the black belt.
I heard the wise old trees of Georgia cry the cry of your
    lynched sons.

I saw the scabrous,
filthy walls of Harlem cry the cry of your clean heart . . .

One day at dawn
I saw the toppled white tombstones of your great
rise and grow
taller than
the tallest lynch trees of your land.
  I saw Paul
standing on the beach—singing
across the sea
I heard his mighty voice, tragic thunder of
man's heart, rearing through the waves. I thought it was
the roaring sea, singing
to our brother, singing to
our might.

(*from* BEHOLD THE SEA)

Plaint

I, Rainey Betha, 22,
From the top branch of race-hatred look at you.
My limbs are bound, though boundless the
    bright sun
Like my bright blood which had to run
Into the orchard that excluded me.
Now I climb death's tree.

The pruninghooks of many mouths
Cut the black-leaved boughs.
The robins of my eyes hover where
Sixteen leaves feel that were a prayer:
Sixteen mouths are open wide,
The minutes, like black cherries,
Drop from my shady side.

Oh who is the forester must tend such a tree, Lord?
Do angels pick the cherry-blood of folk like
    me, Lord?

Unwanted

The poster with my picture on it
Is hanging on the bulletin board in the Post Office.

I stand by it hoping to be recognized
Posing first full face and then profile

But everybody passes by and I have to admit
The photograph was taken some years ago.

I was unwanted then and I'm unwanted now
Ah guess ah'll go up echo mountain and crah.

I wish someone would find my fingerprints somewhere
Maybe on a corpse and say, You're it.

Description: Male, or reasonably so
White, but not lily-white and usually deep-red

Thirty-fivish, and looks it lately
Five-feet-nine and one-hundred-thirty pounds: no physique

Black hair going gray, hairline receding fast
What used to be curly, now fuzzy

Brown eyes starey under beetling brow
Mole on chin, probably will become a wen

It is perfectly obvious that he was not popular at school
No good at baseball, and wet his bed.

His aliases tell his history: Dumbell, Good-for-nothing,
Jewboy, Fieldinsky, Skinny, Fierce Face, Greaseball, Sissy.

Warning: This man is not dangerous, answers to any name
Responds to love, don't call him or he will come.

ALFRED, LORD TENNYSON (1809–92)

I Wage Not Any Feud With Death

I wage not any feud with Death
    For changes wrought on form and face;
    No lower life that earth's embrace
May breed with him can fright my faith.

Eternal process moving on,
    From state to state the spirit walks;
    And these are but the shattered stalks,
Or ruined chrysalis of one.

Nor blame I Death, because he bare
    The use of virtue out of earth;
    I know transplanted human worth
Will bloom to profit, otherwhere.

For this alone on Death I wreak
    The wrath that garners in my heart:
    He put our lives so far apart
We cannot hear each other speak.

EDNA ST. VINCENT MILLAY (1892–1951)

Dirge Without Music

I am not resigned to the shutting away of loving hearts in the
    hard ground.
So it is, and so it will be, for so it has been, time out of mind:
Into the darkness they go, the wise and the lovely. Crowned
With lilies and with laurel they go; but I am not resigned.

Lovers and thinkers, into the earth with you.
Be one with dull, the indiscriminate dust
A fragment of what you felt, of what you knew,
A formula, a phrase remains,—but the best is lost.

The answers quick & keen, the honest look, the laughter, the
    love,
They are gone. They have gone to feed the roses. Elegant and
    curled
Is the blossom. Fragrant is the blossom. I know. But I do not
    approve.
More precious was the light in your eyes than all the roses in
    the world.

Down, down, down into the darkness of the grave
Gently they go, the beautiful, the tender, the kind;
Quietly they go, the intelligent, the witty, the brave.
I know. But I do not approve. And I am not resigned.

Sonnet—To Science

Science! true daughter of Old Time thou art!
  Who alterest all things with thy peering eyes.
Why preyest thou thus upon the poet's heart,
  Vulture, whose wings are dull realities?
How should he love thee? or how deem thee wise,
  Who wouldst not leave him in his wandering
To seek for treasure in the jewelled skies,
  Albeit he soared with an undaunted wing?
Hast thou not dragged Diana from her car,
  And driven the Hamadryad from the wood
To seek a shelter in some happier star?
  Hast thou not torn the Naiad from her flood,
The Elfin from the green grass, and from me
The summer dream beneath the tamarind tree?

Dr. Sigmund Freud Discovers the Sea Shell

Science, that simple saint, cannot be bothered
Figuring what anything is for:
Enough for her devotions that things are
And can be contemplated soon as gathered.

She knows how every living thing was fathered,
She calculated the climate of each star,
She counts the fish at sea, but cannot care
Why any one of them exists, fish, fire or feathered.

Why should she? Her religion is to tell
By rote her rosary of perfect answers.
Metaphysics she can leave to man:
She never wakes at night or heaven or hell

Staring at darkness. In her holy cell
There is no darkness ever: the pure candle
Burns, the beads drop briskly from her hand.

Who dares to offer Her the curled sea shell!
She will not touch it!—knows the world she sees
Is all the world there is! Her faith is perfect!

And still he offers the sea shell. . . .

What surf
Of what far sea upon what unknown ground
Troubles forever with that asking sound?
What surge is this whose question never ceases?

JAMES RUSSELL LOWELL (1819–91)

Ez Fer War

Ez fer war, I call it murder—
    There you hev it plain an' flat;
I don't want to go no furder
    Than my Testyment fer that;
God hez sed so plump an' fairly,
    Et's ez long ez it is broad
An' you've gut to git up airly
    Ef you want to take in God.

'Taint your eppletts an' feathers
    Make the thing a grain more right;
'Taint affollerin' your bell-wethers
    Will excuse ye in his sight;
Ef you take a sword an' drop it,
    An' go stick a feller thru,
Guv'ment aint to answer for it,
    God'll send the bill to you.

Wut's the use o' meetin' goin'
    Every Sabbath, wet or dry,
Ef it's right to go amowin'
    Feller-men like oats an' rye?
I dunno but wut it's pooty
    Trainin' round in bobtail coats,—
But it's curus Christian dooty
    This 'ere cuttin' folks's throats. . . .

Tell ye jest the eend I've come to
    Arter cipherin' plaguy smart,
An' it makes a handy sum, tu
    Any gump could larn by heart;
Laborin' man an' laborin' woman
    Hev one glory an' one shame.
Ev'y thin' that's done inhuman
    Injers all on' em the same. . . .

(*from* THE BIGLOW PAPERS)

83

B-52'S

Against summer, the leaf-lovely wide and lively trees,
The bird songs wild and tanager, the saint's walk,
And the sermon where the brown sparrows toss and talk;
Against the fields' burn of hay and mowers, the degrees
Of meadow upon meadow rising and running far and away;
Against all this, against lovers and the heart's day,
Against daybreak and daylight and holy delight,

They have instrumented death, under and overhead.

I am filtered through by the ooze.
I smell their blind eyes
Touch the child sleeping who does not know.
Like blue flies
They hover against summer.
They lean over and touch the rose dead.

Animals

I think I could turn and live with animals, they are so
    placid and self-contained;
I stand and look at them long and long.
They do not sweat and whine about their condition;
They do not lie awake in the dark and weep for their sins;
They do not make me sick discussing their duty to God;
Not one is dissatisfied—not one is demented with the mania
    of owning things;
Not one kneels to another, nor to his kind that lived
    thousands of years ago;
Not one is respectable or industrious over the whole earth.

The Flower-Fed Buffaloes

The flower-fed buffaloes of the spring
In the days of long ago,
Ranged where the locomotives sing
And the prairie flowers lie low:—
The tossing, blooming, perfumed grass
Is swept away by the wheat,
Wheels and wheels and wheels spin by
In the spring that still is sweet.
But the flower-fed buffaloes of the spring
Left us, long ago.
They gore no more, they bellow no more,
They trundle around the hills no more:—
With the Blackfeet, lying low,
With the Pawnees, lying low
Lying low.

Dover Beach

The sea is calm tonight,
The tide is full, the moon lies fair
Upon the straits;—on the French coast, the light
Gleams and is gone; the cliffs of England stand,
Glimmering and vast, out in the tranquil
    bay.
Come to the window, sweet is the night air!
Only, from the long line of spray
Where the sea meets the moon-blanch'd land,
Listen! You hear the grating roar
Of pebbles which the waves draw back, and
    fling,
At their return, up the high strand,
Begin and cease, and then again begin,
With tremulous cadence slow, and bring
The eternal note of sadness in.

Sophocles long ago
Heard it on the Aegean, and it brought
Into his mind the turbid ebb and flow
Of human misery; we
Find also in the sound a thought,
Hearing it by this distant northern sea.

The Sea of Faith
Was once, too, at the full, and round earth's
    shore
Lay like the folds of a bright girdle furl'd.
But now I only hear
Its melancholy, long, withdrawing roar,
Retreating, to the breath
Of the night-wind, down the vast edges drear
And naked shingles of the world.

Ah, love, let us be true
To one another! for the world, which seems

To lie before us like a land of dreams,
So various, so beautiful, so new,
Hath really neither joy, nor love, nor light,
Nor certitude, nor peace, nor help for pain;
And we are here as on a darkling plain
Swept with confused alarms of struggle and
    flight,
Where ignorant armies clash by night.

New Approach Needed

Should you revisit us,
Stay a little longer,
And get to know the place.
Experience hunger,
Madness, disease and war.
You heard about them, true,
It's different having them.
And what about a go
At sex, marriage, children?
All good, but bringing some
Risk of remorse and pain
And fear of an odd sort:
A sort one should, again,
Feel, not just hear about,
To be qualified as
A human-race expert.
On local life, we trust
The resident witness,
Not the royal tourist.
People have suffered worse
And more durable wrongs
Than you did on that cross
(I know—you won't get me
Up on one of those things)
Without much prospect of
Ascending good as new
On the third day, without
'I die, but man shall live'
As a nice cheering thought.

So, next time, come off it,
And get some service in,
Jack, long before you start
To lay down the old law:
If you still want to then.
Tell your dad that from me.

On the Danger of War

Avert, High Wisdom, never vainly wooed,
This threat of War, that shows a land brain-sick.
When nations gain the pitch where rhetoric
Seems reason they are ripe for cannon's food.
Dark looms the issue though the cause be good,
But with the doubt 'tis our old devil's trick.
O now the down-slope of the lunatic
Illumine lest we redden of that brood.
For not since man in his first view of thee
Ascended to the heavens giving sign
Within him of deep sky and sounded sea,
Did he unforfeiting thy laws transgress;
In peril of his blood his ears incline
To drums whose loudness is their emptiness.

Remembering That Island

Remembering that island lying in the rain
(Lost in the North Pacific, lost in time and the war)
With a terrible fatigue as of repeated dreams
Of running, climbing, fighting in the dark,
I feel the wind rising and the pitiless cold surf
Shaking the headlands of the black north.

And the ships come in again out of the fog—
As real as nightmare I hear the rattle of blocks
When the first boat comes down, the ghostly whisper of feet
At the barge pier—and wild with strain I wait
For the flags of my first war, the remembered faces,
And mine not among them to make the nightmare safe.
Then without words, with a heavy shuffling of gear,
The figures plod in the rain, in the shoreside mud,
Speechless and tired; their faces, lined and hard,
I search for my comrades, and suddenly—there—there—
Harry, Charlie, and Bob, but their faces are worn, old,
And mine is among them. In a dream as real as war

I see the vast stinking Pacific suddenly awash
Once more with bodies, landing on all beaches,
The bodies of dead and living go back to appointed places,
A ten year old resurrection,
And myself once more in the scourging wind, waiting,
    waiting
While the rich oratory and the lying famous corrupt
Senators mine our lives for another war.

"What Soft, Cherubic Creatures"

What soft, cherubic creatures
   These gentlewomen are!
One would as soon assault a plush
   Or violate a star.

Such dimity convictions,
   A horror so refined
Of freckled human nature,
   Of Deity ashamed,—

It's such a common glory,
   A fisherman's degree!
Redemption, 'brittle lady,
   Be so, ashamed of thee.

'The Cambridge Ladies'

the Cambridge ladies who live in furnished souls
are unbeautiful and have comfortable minds
(also, with the Church's protestant blessings
daughters, unscented shapeless spirited)
they believe in Christ and Longfellow, both dead,
are invariably interested in so many things—
at the present writing one still finds
delighted fingers knitting for the is it Poles?
perhaps.   While permanent faces coyly bandy
scandal of Mrs. N and Professor D
. . . . the Cambridge ladies do not care, above
Cambridge if sometimes in its box of
sky lavender and cornerless, the
moon rattles like a fragment of angry candy

Hap

If but some vengeful god would call to me
From up the sky, and laugh: "Thou suffering thing,
Know that thy sorrow is my ecstasy,
That thy love's loss is my hate's profiting!"

Then would I bear it, clench myself, and die,
Steeled by the sense of ire unmerited;
Half-eased in that a Powerfuller than I
Had willed and meted me the tears I shed.

But not so. How arrives it joy lies slain,
And why unblooms the best hope ever sown?
—Crass Casualty obstructs the sun and rain,
And dicing Time for gladness casts a moan. . . .
These purblind Doomsters had as readily strown
Blisses about my pilgrimage as pain.

The Orb Weaver

Here is the spinner, the orb weaver,
Devised of jet, embossed with sulphur,
Hanging among the fruits of summer,

Hour after hour serenely sullen,
Ripening as September ripens,
Plumping like a grape or melon.

And in its winding-sheet the grasshopper.

The art, the craftsmanship, the cunning,
The patience, the self-control, the waiting,
The sudden dart and the needled poison.

I have no quarrel with the spider
But with the mind or mood that made her
To thrive in nature and in man's nature.

Channel Firing

That night your great guns, unawares,
Shook all our coffins as we lay,
And broke the chancel window-squares,
We thought it was the Judgment-day

And sat upright. While drearisome
Arose the howl of wakened hounds:
The mouse let fall the altar-crumb,
The worms drew back into the mounds,

The glebe cow drooled. Till God called, "No;
It's gunnery practice out at sea
Just as before you went below;
The world is as it used to be:

"All nations striving strong to make
Red war yet redder. Mad as hatters
They do no more for Christés sake
Than you who are helpless in such matters.

"That this is not the judgment hour
For some of them's a blessed thing,
For if it were they'd have to scour
Hell's floor for so much threatening. . . .

"Ha, ha. It will be warmer when
I blow the trumpet (if indeed
I ever do; for you are men,
And rest eternal sorely need)."

So down we lay again. "I wonder,
Will the world ever saner be,"
Said one, "than when He sent us under
In our indifferent century!"

And many a skeleton shook his head.
"Instead of preaching forty year,"
My neighbour Parson Thirdly said,
"I wish I had stuck to pipes and beer."

Again the guns disturbed the hour,
Roaring their readiness to avenge
As far inland as Stourton Tower,
And Camelot, and starlit Stonehenge.

It Is Not Enough

. . . It is not enough
to photograph the South Vietnam Premier
in a new BVD tee shirt
it does not give the populace assurance
that a WIN policy is in effect
We need THE WAR LEAGUE OF NATIONS!!

This League will need a fifty-mile-square
area fenced off (the fences can carry advertising
            which will give the LEAGUE additional revenues
            but more importantly this will also give
            the American Businessmen a sense of participation
            outside of armaments)

There will be two divisions:
The Guerilla League & The Air Combat League
TV Cameras and radio microphones will be situated
at strategic locations
and will have complete mobility at all times

Media crews will be identified
by red crosses
Mickey Mantle will be Commissioner of War

Special Sightseeing concerns are invited
& Mr. Robert Moses has been assured
that opening day will occur
adjacent to the World's Fair

Each General must be given equal time
for "on the field" interviews

In the event
of a great feat
or major victory
the barracks of the lucky Army
must be thrown open to Media

Every five years
we will have a World Series
between the Guerilla-congs
& the air combat bombers
low-yield Atomic Bombs will be allowed
along with poison gases

Red China is not allowed in the league
unless she attacks . . .

(*from a Prospectus on the New War League of Nations
to Be Distributed to All Major TV/Radio Media*)

GERARD MANLEY HOPKINS (1844–89)

Spring and Fall
(to a Young Child)

Márgarét, are you griéving
Over Goldengrove unleaving?
Leáves, líke the things of man, you
With your fresh thoughts care for, can you?
Áh! ás the heart grows older
It will come to such sights colder
By and by, nor spare a sigh
Though worlds of wanwood leafmeal lie;
And yet you will weep and know why.
Now no matter, child, the name:
Sórrow's spríngs áre the same,
Nor mouth had, no nor mind, expressed
What heart heard of, ghost guessed:
It is the blight man was born for,
It is Margaret you mourn for.

WILLIAM BUTLER YEATS *(1865–1939)*

The Lamentation of the Old Pensioner

Although I shelter from the rain
Under a broken tree,
My chair was nearest to the fire
In every company
That talked of love or politics,
Ere Time transfigured me.

Though lads are making pikes again
For some conspiracy,
And crazy rascals rage their fill
At human tyranny,
My contemplations are of Time
That has transfigured me.

There's not a woman turns her face
Upon a broken tree,
And yet the beauties that I loved
Are in my memory;
I spit into the face of Time
That has transfigured me.

EDWIN ARLINGTON ROBINSON (1869-1935)

Cassandra

I heard one who said: 'Verily,
  What word have I for children here?
Your Dollar is your only Word,
  The wrath of it, your only fear.

'You build it altars tall enough
  To make you see, but you are blind;
You cannot leave it long enough
  To look before you or behind.

'When Reason beckons you to pause,
  You laugh and say that you know best;
But what it is you know, you keep
  As dark as ingots in a chest.

'You laugh and answer, "We are young;
  O leave us now, and let us grow."—
Not asking how much more of this
  Will Time endure or Fate bestow.

'Because a few complacent years
  Have made your peril of your pride,
Think you that you are to go on
  Forever pampered and untried?

'What lost eclipse of history,
  What bivouac of the marching stars,
Has given the sign for you to see
  Millenniums and last great wars?

'What unrecorded overthrow
  Of all the world has ever known,
Or ever been, has made itself
  So plain to you, and you alone?

'Your Dollar, Dove, and Eagle make
  A Trinity that even you

Rate higher than you rate yourselves;
    It pays, it flatters, and it's new.

'And though your very flesh and blood
    Be what your Eagle eats and drinks,
You'll praise him for the best of birds,
    Not knowing what the Eagle thinks.

'The power is yours, but not the sight;
    You see not upon what you tread;
You have the ages for your guide,
    But not the wisdom to be led.

'Think you to tread forever down
    The merciless old verities?
And are you never to have eyes
    To see the world for what it is?

'Are you to pay for what you have
    With all you are?'—No other word
We caught, but with a laughing crowd
    Moved on. None heeded, and few heard.

This Morning The Sun

This morning the sun
for the first time in 7,000,000 years
reported late
for work.
A major disaster was declared,
the mayor crawled underneath Manhattan
with his Mark Cross survival kit,
governments in Saigon
chased each other through revolving doors,
molten metal fell from the eyes of Bartholdi's Statue,
which went public and was sold at noon
on the Stock Exchange.

> Leaving our dinosaur footprints through
> the streets of cities,
> what future tarpits will reveal our
> bones?
> What amber of what eye
> preserve this age?

Sheriff Rainey shifted his plug
of Red Man tobacco
and spat clear to Washington,
staining the White House and the white walls of the
Capitol
with dark runnels of derision.
Whose blood? Whose Blood
on the Lincoln Monument?
Chaney's. Goodman's. Schwerner's.
They are dragging Walt Whitman through the streets
of Mississippi.
(Bearded Jew from Brooklyn.)
They've got a rope around Abe Lincoln's neck.
(What'd we do that's wrong if we
killed two Jews and one Nigger?)

> Then all the ovens of Maidanek
> opened their mouths.

I saw the enemy, a seven-year-old boy.
I heard him screaming for his cooked
                                    eyeballs.
I saw the granny blazing like a bundle
                            of reeds,
heard the infant wailing in a winding-sheet
                            of flame
in a village of thatched huts
hit by napalm.

The stones hate us.
The eyes are bitter.
Every tree is out to strangle us.
The grass mistrusts us.
We are strangers here at a million bucks a day.
They say the richest man in the world has just
foreclosed Fort Knox.
A million bucks a day can buy
a President. A war. A world.
          But not one hair of the head of the
              seven-year-old boy
          in a village that went up in napalm.

(*from* ANOTHER LATE EDITION)

RALPH   HODGSON   (1872–   )

The Bells of Heaven

'Twould ring the bells of Heaven
The wildest peal for years
If Parson lost his senses
And people came to theirs,
And he and they together
Knelt down with angry prayers
For tamed and shabby tigers,
And dancing dogs and bears,
And wretched, blind pit ponies,
And little hunted hares.

Counting the Mad

This one was put in a jacket,
This one was sent home,
This one was given bread and meat
But would eat none,
And this one cried No No No No
All day long.

This one looked at the window
As though it were a wall,
This one saw things that were not there,
This one things that were,
And this one cried No No No No
All day long.

This one thought himself a bird,
This one a dog,
And this one thought himself a man,
An ordinary man,
And cried and cried No No No No
All day long.

Petit, the Poet

Seeds in a dry pod, tick, tick, tick,
Tick, tick, tick, like mites in a quarrel—
Faint iambics that the full breeze wakens—
But the pine tree makes a symphony thereof.
Triolets, villanelles, rondels, rondeaus,
Ballades by the score with the same old thought:
The snows and the roses of yesterday are vanished;
And what is love but a rose that fades?
Life all around me here in the village:
Tragedy, comedy, valor and truth,
Courage, constancy, heroism, failure—
All in the loom, and oh what patterns!
Woodlands, meadows, streams and rivers—
Blind to all of it all my life long.
Triolets, villanelles, rondels, rondeaus,
Seeds in a dry pod, tick, tick, tick,
Tick, tick, tick, what little iambics,
While Homer and Whitman roared in the pines!

The Line of an American Poet

That American Poet's future
Was bright because he began
With the know-how of Ford and Chrysler
And the faith of American Can.

He fathomed success's secret
And stuck to his P's and Q's
And urged himself, over and over
To produce and produce and produce.

His very first models were cleverly
Built; the market boomed.
Some of the world's most critical
Consumers looked, and consumed.

Lines off his line came smoother
And smoother as more and more
Know-how came in the window
And verses rolled out the door,

Until everyone in the market
Knew that his new works were sure
To be just what the country had need of:
Poems uniform, safe and sure.

The Man With the Hoe

> (God made man in His own image
> In the image of God made He him.—GENESIS)

Bowed by the weight of centuries he leans
Upon his hoe and gazes on the ground,
The emptiness of ages in his face,
And on his back the burden of the world.
Who made him dead to rapture and despair,
A thing that grieves not and that never hopes,
Stolid and stunned, a brother to the ox?
Who loosened and let down this brutal jaw?
Whose was the hand that slanted back this brow?
Whose breath blew out the light within this brain?

Is this the Thing the Lord God made and gave
To have dominion over sea and land;
To trace the stars and search the heavens for power;
To feel the passion of Eternity?
Is this the dream He dreamed who shaped the suns
And markt their ways upon the ancient deep?
Down all the caverns of Hell to their last gulf
There is no shape more terrible than this—
More tongued with censure of the world's blind greed—
More filled with signs and portents for the soul—
More packt with danger to the universe.

What gulfs between him and the seraphim!
Slave of the wheel of labor, what to him
Are Plato and the swing of Pleiades?
What the long reaches of the peaks of song,
The rife of dawn, the reddening of the rose?
Through this dread shape the suffering ages look;
Time's tragedy is in that aching stoop;
Through this dread shape humanity betrayed,
Plundered, profaned and disinherited,
Cries protest to the Powers that make the world,
A protest that is also prophecy.

O masters, lords and rulers in all lands,
Is this the handiwork you give to God,
This monstrous thing distorted and soul-quencht?
How will you ever straighten up this shape;
Touch it again with immortality;
Give back the upward looking and the light;
Rebuild in it the music and the dream;
Make right the immemorial infamies,
Perfidious wrongs, immedicable woes?

O masters, lords and rulers in all lands,
How will the future reckon with this Man?
How answer his brute question in that hour
When whirlwinds of rebellion shake all shores?
How will it be with kingdoms and with kings—
With those who shaped him to the thing he is—
When this dumb Terror shall rise to judge the world,
After the silence of the centuries?

Landscape Near a Steel Mill

Over the books of bricks,
over the vague meanings of dust—
with a taste of leather,
with a rough static of purple, like wine—
entering the empty houses at evening,
the slow circumference of supper hangs out
its banner of striped shadow.

Wallets are closed;
cars start up
like an uprising of lions,
and the furnaces fall into themselves
like a pillow of autumn leaves,
and, with a great sigh of a dead bagpipe,
become in silence, passive sunsets.

How shall I tell you
of all the doors I came upon?
Of the small shredded joys
that cried in paper tears,
and how I saw silence
come down in parachutes of fire?

Yes, all things revolt against
the dying static of sunlight.
Only the bankers are left,
polishing their interest globes
through the long night,
milking their beards
like magicians pulling out quarters
from the combinations of air.

But I shall tell you of the dusty children:
I saw them
scraped through the back of a yawn:
wave-lifted,

their birds flying paper joys,
uncertain in a square of uncertainty,
but echoing in their tinny valleys, galloping hearts.
And I saw hands like
lighted menorahs on the horizon
foreseeing future sunrises,

crying: Fools! Where is our bread?

EZRA POUND (1885–)

Ancient Music

Winter is icummen in,
Lhude sing Goddamm,
Raineth drop and staineth slop,
And how the wind doth ramm!
     Sing: Goddamm.
Skiddeth bus and sloppeth us,
An ague hath my ham.
Freezeth river, turneth liver,
     Damn you, sing: Goddamm.
Goddamm, Goddamm, 'tis why I am, Goddamm,
     So 'gainst the winter's balm.
Sing goddamm, damm, sing Goddamm,
Sing goddamm, sing goddamm, DAMM.

Late Late

Where tomahawks flash in the powwow
and tommyguns deepen the hubbub
and panzers patrol, is the horror
I live without sleep for the love of,

whose A-bombs respond to the tom-tom,
whose halberds react to the ack-ack,
while I, as if slugged with a dumdum,
sit back and sit back and sit back

until the last gunman is drawn on,
last murderous rustler druv loco,
last prisoncamp commandant spat at,
and somehow, and poco a poco,

the bottles are gone from the sixpack,
sensation is gone from the buttocks,
Old Glory dissolves into static,
the box is a box is a box.

I Sing of Olaf

i sing of Olaf glad and big
whose warmest heart recoiled at war:
a conscientious object-or

his well-beloved colonel (trig
westpointer most succinctly bred)
took erring Olaf soon in hand;
but—though an host of overjoyed
noncoms (first knocking on the head
him) do through icy waters roll
that helplessness which others stroke
with brushes recently employed
anent this muddy toiletbowl,
while kindred intellects evoke
allegiance per blunt instruments—
Olaf (being to all intents
a corpse and wanting any rag
upon what God unto him gave)
responds, without getting annoyed
"I will not kiss your f.ing flag"

straightway the silver bird looked grave
(departing hurriedly to shave)

but—though all kinds of officers
(a yearning nation's blueeyed pride)
their passive prey did kick and curse
until for wear their clarion
voices and boots were much the worse,
and egged the firstclassprivates on
his rectum wickedly to tease
by means of skilfully applied
bayonets roasted hot with heat—
Olaf (upon what were once knees)
does almost ceaselessly repeat

"there is some s. I will not eat"

our president, being of which
assertions duly notified
threw the yellowsonofabitch
into a dungeon, where he died

Christ (of His mercy infinite)
i pray to see; and Olaf, too

preponderatingly because
unless statistics lie he was
more brave than me: more blond than you.

Recruiting Drive

Under the willow the willow
    I heard the butcher-bird sing,
Come out you fine young fellow
    From under your mother's wing.
I'll show you the magic garden
    That hangs in the beamy air,
The way of the lynx and the angry Sphinx
    And the fun of the freezing fair.

Lie down lie down with my daughter
    Beneath the Arabian tree,
Gaze on your face in the water
    Forget the scribbling sea.
Your pillow the nine bright shiners
    Your bed the spilling sand,
But the terrible toy of my lily-white boy
    Is the gun in his innocent hand.

You must take off your clothes for the doctor
    And stand as straight as a pin
His hand of stone on your white breast-bone
    Where the bullets all go in.
They'll dress you in lawn and linen
    And fill you with Plymouth gin,
O the devil may wear a rose in his hair
    I'll wear my fine doe-skin

My mother weeps as I leave her
    But I tell her it won't be long,
The murderers wail in Wandsworth Gaol
    But I shoot a more popular song.
Down in the enemy country
    Under the enemy tree
There lies a lad whose heart has gone bad
    Waiting for me, for me.

He says I have no culture
    And that when I've stormed the pass
I shall fall on the farm with a smoking arm
    And ravish his bonny lass.
Under the willow the willow
    Death spreads her dripping wings
And caught in the snare of the bleeding air
    The butcher-bird sings, sings, sings.

✗ —Conformity

THEODORE ROETHKE (1908–63)

Dolour

I have known the inexorable sadness of pencils,
Neat in their boxes, dolour of pad and paper-weights,
All the misery of manilla folders and mucilage,
Desolation in immaculate public places,
Lonely reception rooms, lavatory, switchboard,
The unalterable pathos of basin and pitcher,
Ritual of multigraph, paper-clip, comma,
Endless duplication of lives and objects,
And I have seen dust from the walls of institutions,
Finer than flour, alive, more dangerous than silica,
Sift, almost invisible, through long afternoons of tedium,
Dropping a fine film on nails and delicate eyebrows,
Glazing the pale hair, the duplicate grey standard faces.

Borderline Ballad

Bring out all the set ideas.
Cram them into a giant saucepan.
Boil and stir them to a porridge
To clog and cloy the guts of man.

Record the pomp and fury
Of premiers, presidents and those
Whose voices when they speak to us
Sound like the blowing of a nose.

Take down the books of essays,
Philosophical, psychological, socio-
Logical and all the other logicals;
Priestlike, perform a great lavabo.

Come back again in a hundred years
Filled with faith, hope and clarity
And tell me then if you'll not find
The whole lot's back in quantity.

Award

[A Gold Watch to the FBI Man (who has followed me)
for 25 Years.]

Well, old spy
looks like I
led you down some pretty blind alleys,
took you on several trips to Mexico,
fishing in the high Sierras,
jazz at the Philharmonic.
You've watched me all your life,
I've clothed your wife,
put your two sons through college.
what good has it done?
sun keeps rising every morning.
Ever see me buy an Assistant President?
or close a school?
or lend money to Somoza?
I bought some after-hours whiskey in L.A.
but the Chief got his pay.
I ain't killed no Koreans,
or fourteen-year-old boys in Mississippi
neither did I bomb Guatemala,
or lend guns to shoot Algerians.
I admit I took a Negro child
to a white rest room in Texas,
but she was my daughter, only three,
and she had to pee,
and I just didn't know what to do,
would you?
see, I'm so light, it don't seem right
to go the colored rest room;
my daughter's brown, and folks frown on that in Texas,
I just don't know how to go to the bathroom in the free world!

Now, old FBI man,
you've done the best you can,
you lost me a few jobs,

scared a couple landlords,
You got me struggling for that bread,
but I ain't dead.
and before it's all through,
I may be following you!

Speech to the Court

Even now the question has changed since I started this
  summation to the jury. How can we arrive at an honest
  verdict? The crime consists in going on
  trial in the first place.
We should all be declared innocent by birth.
You get the drift? You answer the question and I will
  always find a new one and we will go arm in arm
  down the airways singing Happy Birthdays.
But don't ask me to pull the Trujillo bullet from your brain,
  the Nazi needle from your heart; put out the
  White Citizens' fire toasting your feet or
  extract the Strontium 90 from your bones.
Once we start that kind of business the bleeding begins
  and we commit the unforgivable sentimentality—as if
  a handcuff were latched to our fossil skins and
  we grinned up at the anthropologist who discovered us
  at the fireside where we were heartbeats loving each
  other so sweetly in the kitchen middens we can't
  forget.
We are not desperate—that passed with the first mushroom
  when the Pentagon said to God: "Let there be
  clouds" and we all started singing Peace.
It's not a choice between madness and suicide—
  that's only the way it appears. The choice
  historically is to be heard or not to be heard;
  to accept the vast silence around us or to
  scream intelligibly.
Just believe in sunshine up to the limits of your
  benefits under the Unemployment System and you
  will smile like bacon cracklings in the morning
  happily forever after. . . .
                          —for our eyes see ahead
                            and we know we are moving
                            towards the songs of others.

Security

Filthy, sick, and dying,
They wait, they mill and wait
Beyond the farther gate
Of our denying.

And here, within the city,
They, too, we safely lock
In slum or cage who mock
Us. Waste no pity.

If shadows stalk each pleasure
And nightmares batter dreams,
If horror glares, and screams
Rise out of measure,

The guard, be sure, is armed;
Full-practised now, though few,
They know what they're to do.
Don't be alarmed.

We've cast out every devil,
Not one left, crying love.
Oh, at the gates, they move,
But—fear no evil.

Give Way

Give way to the man coming at you:
He is probably organized, or he
Is a Mason, so much the worse
For you. The child ahead of you
Walks carefully, does not step
On a crack. She knows. Keep
Close to the buildings, stick
To the well-lit avenues, give way.

"Man that is born of woman is of
Few days, and full of trouble.
He cometh forth like a flower,
And is cut down: he fleeth also
As a shadow, and continueth not."
Your path will be covered with cracks;
Beware of a tall man who will bring
Ill fortune; beware of a short man:
He will be armed.

            Or, better yet,
Organize, call meetings, make speeches,
Pay dues. With the dues, acquire
A public address system, and make
Louder speeches. Cast ballots, win.

If you will notice, now, the tall
Man, he tests the microphones,
The short man insures with his gun
The collection of dues; everyone
Is stepping between the cracks.
However, nobody is fully satisfied:
Keep close to the buildings, give way;
The man coming at you may be armed.

Examiner

The routine trickery of the examination
Baffles these hot and discouraged youths.
Driven by they know not what external pressure
They pour their hated self-analysis
Through the nib of confession, onto the accusatory page.

I, who have plotted their immediate downfall,
I am entrusted with the divine categories,
ABCD and the hell of E,
The parade of prize and the backdoor of pass.

In the tight silence
Standing by the green grass window
Watching the fertile earth graduate its sons
With more compassion—not commanding the shape
Of stem and stamen, bringing the trees to pass
By shift of sunlight and increase of rain,
For each seed the whole soil, for the inner life
The environment receptive and contributory—
I shudder at the narrow frames of our text-book schools
In which we plant our so various seedlings.
Each brick-walled barracks
Cut into numbered rooms, black-boarded,
Ties the venturing shoot to the master stick;
The screw-desk rows of lads and girls
Subdued in the shade of an adult—
Their acid subsoil—
Shape the new to the old in the ashen garden.
Shall we open the whole skylight of thought
To these tiptoe minds, bring them our frontier worlds
And the boundless uplands of art for their field of
    growth?

Or shall we pass them the chosen poems with the foot-
    notes,
Ring the bell on their thoughts, period their play,

Make laws for averages and plans for means,
Print one history book for a whole province, and
Let ninety thousand reach page 10 by Tuesday?

As I gather the inadequate paper evidence, I hear
Across the neat campus lawn
The professional mowers drone, clipping the inch-high
   green.

A Poem to Delight My Friends
Who Laugh at Science-Fiction

That was the year
the small birds in their frail and delicate battalions
committed suicide against the Empire State,
having, in some never-explained manner,
lost their aerial radar, or ignored it.

That was the year
men and women everywhere stopped dying natural deaths.
The aged, facing sleep, took poison;
the infant, facing life, died with the mother in childbirth;
and the whole wild remainder of the population,
despairing but deliberate, crashed in auto accidents
on roads as clear and uncluttered as ponds.

That was the year every ship on every ocean,
every lake, harbor, river, vanished without trace;
and even ships docked at quays
turned over like wounded animals, harpooned whales, on
      Normandies.

Yes, and the civilian transcontinental planes
found, like the war-planes, the sky-lanes crowded
and, praising Icarus, plunged to earth in flames.

Many, mild stay-at-homes, slipped in bathtubs,
others, congenital indoors-men, descending stairs,
and some, irrepressible roisterers, playing musical chairs.
Tots fell from scooter cars and tricycles
and casual passersby were stabbed by falling icicles.

Ah, what carnage! It was reported
that even bicarb and aspirin turned fatal,
and seconal too, to those with mild headaches,
whose stomachs were slightly acid, or who found they
      could not sleep.
All lovers died in bed, as all seafarers on the deep.

Till finally the only people left alive
were the soldiers sullenly spread on battlefields
among the shell-pocked hills and the charred trees.
Thus, even the indispensable wars died of ennui.

But not the expendable conscripts: they remained as always.
However, since no transport was available anywhere,
and home, in any case, was dead, and bare,
the soldiers wandered eternally
in their dazed, early-Chirico landscapes,
Like drunken stars in their shrinking orbits
round and round and round and round

and (since I too died in the world-wide suicide)
they may still, for all I know, be there.
Like forsaken chessmen abandoned by paralyzed players,
they may still be there,
may still be there.

prologue

Strong Men

They dragged you from homeland,
They chained you in coffles,
They huddled you spoon-fashion in filthy hatches,
They sold you to give a few gentlemen ease.

They broke you in like oxen,
They scourged you,
They branded you,
They made your women breeders,
They swelled your numbers with bastards . . .
They taught you the religion they disgraced.

You sang:
  Keep a-inchin' along
  Lak a po' inch worm . . .

You sang:
  Bye and bye
  I'm gonna lay down dis heaby load . . .

You sang:
  Walk togedder, chillen,
  Dontcha git weary . . .

    The strong men keep a-comin' on
    The strong men git stronger.

They point with pride to the roads you built for them,
They ride in comfort over the rails you laid for them.
They put hammers in your hands
And said—Drive so much before sundown.

You sang:
  Ain't no hammah
  In dis lan'
  Strikes lak mine, bebby,
  Strikes lak mine.

127

They cooped you in their kitchens,
They penned you in their factories,
They gave you the jobs that they were too good for,
They tried to guarantee happiness to themselves
By shunting dirt and misery to you.

You sang:
   Me an' muh baby gonna shine, shine
   Me an' muh baby gonna shine.
      The strong men keep a-comin' on
      The strong men git stronger . . .

They bought off some of your leaders
You stumbled, as blind men will . . .
They coaxed you, unwontedly soft-voiced . . .
You followed a way.
Then laughed as usual.
They heard the laugh and wondered;
Uncomfortable;
Unadmitting a deeper terror . . .
      The strong men keep a-comin' on
      Gittin' stronger . . .

What, from the slums
Where they have hemmed you,
What, from the tiny huts
They could not keep from you—
What reaches them
Making them ill at ease, fearful?
Today they shout prohibition at you
"Thou shalt not this"
"Thou shalt not that"
"Reserved for whites only"
You laugh.

One thing they cannot prohibit—
      The strong men . . . coming on
      The strong men gittin' stronger.
      Strong men . . .
      Stronger . . .

We Didn't Know

We didn't know, said the burgermeister
About the camp on the edge of town.
It was Hitler and his crew
That tore the German nation down.
We saw the cattle cars, it's true;
Maybe they carried a Jew or two.
They woke us up as they rattled through.
But what did you expect me to do?

We didn't know at all, we didn't see a thing.
You can't hold us to blame, what could we do?
It was a terrible shame but we can't bear the blame.
Oh no, not us, we didn't know.

We didn't know, said the congregation
Singing a hymn in their church of white.
The press was full of lies about us,
Preacher told us we were right.
The outside agitators came—
They burned some churches and put the blame
On decent southern people's name
To set our colored people aflame.
And maybe some of our boys got hot
And a couple of niggers and reds got shot.
They should have stayed where they belong,
The preacher would have told us if we'd done wrong.

We didn't know, said the puzzled voter,
Watching the president on T.V.
I guess we got to drop those bombs
If we're going to keep south Asia free.
The president is such a peaceful man
I guess he's got some kind of plan.
They're saying we've tortured prisoners of war,
But I don't believe that stuff no more.

Torturing prisoners is a communist game,
And you can bet they're doing the same.
I wish this war was over and through,
But what do you expect me to do?

A Hiroshima Lullaby

for Sadako Sasaki, dead of leukemia in October 1955 at the age of twelve. A few months before her death she tried to fold 1,000 paper cranes, which according to Japanese legend would protect her health; she had reached 964 when she died. Her childhood classmates completed the magic thousand and raised the money for her statue, holding a golden folded crane, in the Peace Park in Hiroshima.

Sadako, you have gone
beyond the fire's fear;
we follow where you walk
upon that magic hill.

The Hiroshima birds
come back across the sea
into the city square.
Sleep now, Sadako, sleep.

Now on the darkest night
the shadows on the waves
lift from your fallen eyes
upon a cloud of cranes.

They march across the sky,
a thousand in a line
to keep their watch upon
the children in their dreams.

Sadako, here's a star
to cradle in your hand
and fly around the sun
and nest upon the moon.

Sadako, paper girl,
ride on your thousand wings
and cry your gentle prayer.
We fold your paper cranes.

WILLIAM BLAKE (1757–1827)

Jerusalem (from Milton)

And did those feet in ancient time
    Walk upon England's mountains green?
And was the holy Lamb of God
    On England's pleasant pastures seen?

And did the Countenance Divine
    Shine forth upon our clouded hills?
And was Jerusalem builded here
    Among these dark Satanic Mills?

Bring me my bow of burning gold!
    Bring me my arrows of desire!
Bring me my spear! O clouds, unfold!
    Bring me my chariot of fire!

I will not cease from mental fight,
    Nor shall my sword sleep in my hand,
Till we have built Jerusalem
    In England's green and pleasant land.

NOTES ON THE POETS

AESCHYLUS (c. 525–456 B.C.)
Born near Athens. Fought in the Persian wars. The most creative of the Athenian dramatists.

KINGSLEY AMIS (1922–)
Born in London. He has published four novels and three books of verse.

MATTHEW ARNOLD (1822–88)
A poet, yet one better known as a literary critic and interpreter of cultural history.

W. H. AUDEN (1907–)
During the thirties he was the leader of the leftist Oxford poets. He came to America in 1939 and became an American citizen; won the Pulitzer Prize in 1948 for *The Age of Anxiety*.

WILLIAM BLAKE (1757–1827)
Son of a London hosier. Poet, engraver, illustrator, religious mystic.

STERLING BROWN (1901–)
Born in Washington, D.C. Educated at Williams College and Harvard. Distinguished teacher at Howard University. His books include: *Southern Road* (1932), *The Negro in American Fiction* (1938), *Negro Poetry and Drama* (1938).

OLGA CABRAL (20th Century)
Born in the West Indies; now lives in New York. "Another Late Edition" is from a forthcoming book, *The Evaporated Man*.

CHARLES CAUSLEY (1917–)
Born in England. Author of *Survivor's Leave* and *Farewell, Aggie Weston*.

DAVID CLARK (1920–)
Born in Seymour, Connecticut. Yeats scholar, Quaker, he is a member of the English faculty at the University of Massachusetts.

SARAH N. CLEGHORN (1876–1959)
Born in Norfolk, Virginia. Poet, novelist, protestor for social causes.

GEORGE CRABBE (1754–1832)
English poet and clergyman, he opened up the seamy side of English country life in *The Village*, *The Parish Register*, and *The Borough*.

E. E. CUMMINGS (1894–1962)
Born in Cambridge, Massachusetts. Educated at Harvard. Experimentalist in poetry, his books include *XLI Poems* (1925), *Is 5* (1926), *Poems 1923–1954* (1954), and the novel *The Enormous Room* (1922).

EMILY DICKINSON (1830–86)

Born in Amherst, Massachusetts. She wrote more than two thousand poems, almost all of them short, cryptic, and mystical.

JOHN DONNE (1572–1631)

The greatest of the 17th-century metaphysical poets and one of the greatest Anglican divines.

RAY DUREM (1915–63)

Born in Seattle, Washington. A veteran of the Spanish Civil War, he lived in many parts of the United States and Mexico.

TIMOTHY DWIGHT (1752–1817)

Born in Northampton, Massachusetts. A minister, writer, and educator. His poetry takes the form of solemn satire, minor poems, and hymns.

RALPH WALDO EMERSON (1803–82)

Lecturer, essayist, poet, and transcendentalist.

LAWRENCE FERLINGHETTI (1919–)

Born in New York. Reached San Francisco, 1951; built a bookstore. His books include *Coney Island of the Mind* (1958); a novel, *Her* (1960); and a book of plays, *Unfair Arguments with Existence* (1963).

EDWARD FIELD (1924–)

Born in Brooklyn, New York. Grew up in Lynbrook, Long Island. Now living in New York. Won Lamont Award, 1962. Author of book of poems, *Stand Up, Friend, With Me,* 1963.

DONALD FINKEL (1929–)

Born in New York City. He has published in various periodicals and anthologies, and a book of poems, *The Clothing's New Emperor.*

CHARLES HENRI FORD (1913–)

Born in Mississippi. He edited two avant-garde magazines. In recent years he has resided in Paris and Rome.

ROBERT FRANCIS (1900–)

Born in Pennsylvania. Makes his home in Fort Juniper in Amherst, Massachusetts. His books include one novel and six volumes of poetry, the most recent, *Come Out into the Sun.*

PHILIP FRENEAU (1752–1832)

Son of a wealthy New York merchant. Educated at Princeton. Chief poet propagandist of our Revolution.

JOHN GAY (1685–1732)

Playwright and satirist, known best for his *The Fables* and his celebrated parody of Italian opera, *The Beggar's Opera.*

OLIVER GOLDSMITH (1728–74)

Born in Ireland. Famous for *The Vicar of Wakefield* (1766), *The Deserted Village* (1770), and the play *She Stoops to Conquer* (1771).

THOMAS HARDY (1840–1928)

One of the great English novelists. Hardy also wrote bleak, almost angular, yet compassionate poetry.

DAVID HENDERSON (1943–)
Born in Harlem, New York. Author of *Felix of the Silent Forest*.

JOE HILL (1879–1915)
Born in Sweden. In 1910 joined the IWW—the Wobblies. Famous for writing workers' songs. Rebel and artist, he was executed "for murder" in November, 1915.

RALPH HODGSON (1872–1962)
Born in Yorkshire, England. Died at Minerva, Ohio. Works include: *The Last Blackbird* and *Other Lines* (1907), *Poems* (1917), *Silver Wedding* (1941).

THOMAS HOOD (1798–1845)
English writer of light, humorous verse and parodies, yet interested in the social ills of his time.

GERARD MANLEY HOPKINS (1844–89)
Educated at Oxford, Converted to Roman Catholicism in 1866. Jesuit priest. His poems were first collected and published by his friend Robert Bridges in 1918.

HERSCHEL HORN (20th Century)
Born in Detroit, he was brought up on the West Coast, and now lives in New York where he teaches school. He has published a number of poems in magazines.

VICTOR HUGO (1802–95)
Major poet and novelist in 19th-century France.

JEREMIAH (c. 650–? B.C.)
The last of the great pre-exilic prophets of Israel.

JOB (6th Century B.C.)
The Book of Job in the Bible is a work of poetic genius expressing the doubts aroused by undeserved suffering.

DONALD JUSTICE (1925–)
Born in Florida. He is the author of *Summer Anniversaries* (1960) and *Night Light* (1967).

ARNOLD KENSETH (1915–)
Born in Milton, Massachusetts. Has published *A Cycle of Praise* (1952), *The Holy Merriment* (1963). Won the American Scholar Award in 1959. Presently a Congregational minister in Amherst and lecturer in English at the University of Massachusetts.

GALWAY KINNELL (1927–)
Born in Providence, Rhode Island; now living in New York. His published works include *What a Kingdom It Was* (1961), *Flower Herding on Mount Monadnock* (1964), and *Body Rags* (1968).

STANLEY KUNITZ (1905–)
Born in Worcester, Massachusetts. Editor and author of many books, among them *Selected Poems, 1928–1958*.

AARON KURTZ (1891–1964)
Born in Osve, Russia. Lived in New York since childhood and published seven volumes of poetry in Yiddish.

JOSEPH LANGLAND (1917–)
Born in Minnesota. Brought up in Iowa. Co-author of two an-

thologies, *The Short Story*, with James B. Hall, and *Poet's Choice*, with Paul Engle. His latest book of poems is *The Wheel of Summer* (1963).

WILLIAM LANGLAND (c. 1332–c. 1400)
Probable author of *Piers Plowman*, though the poem represents not so much a man as a tradition—the peasant of the later Middle Ages making his voice heard.

CARL LARSEN (1935–   )
Born in Hermosa Beach, California. His first book was *The Plot to Assassinate the Chase National Bank*.

DENISE LEVERTOV (1923–   )
Born in England; now lives in New York. Her books include *With Eyes at the Back of Our Heads* (1959); *O Taste and See* (1964).

VACHEL LINDSAY (1879–1931)
Born in Springfield, Illinois. Principal works: *General William Booth Enters into Heaven* (1913); *The Congo* (1914); *Collected Poems* (1923).

HENRY WADSWORTH LONGFELLOW (1807–82)
Born in Portland, Maine. Taught at Bowdoin and Harvard. His poems, sentimental, often didactic, also revealed his hatred of slavery.

JAMES RUSSELL LOWELL (1819–91)
In his lifetime, professor at Harvard, editor of the *Atlantic Monthly*, and minister to Spain and England.

WALTER LOWENFELS (1897–   )
Born in New York, now living in Peekskill, N.Y. Books in print include *To an Imaginary Daughter, Walt Whitman's Civil War, Some Deaths, Robert Gover's the Portable Walter*; anthologies include *Where Is Vietnam?* and *Poets of Today*.

ARCHIBALD MACLEISCH (1892–   )
Lawyer, poet, dramatist, Assistant Secretary of State, he has won both the Bollingen Prize and the Pulitzer Prize. Among his books are *Collected Poems, 1917–1952* (1952) and the successful Broadway verse play *J.B.*

EDWIN MARKHAM (1852–1940)
Born in Oregon. Schoolteacher and poet. His verses express outrage at social injustice.

EDGAR LEE MASTERS (1869–1950)
Born in Garnett, Kansas. Was brought up in Lewistown, Illinois, the Spoon River country he later made famous in his best-known work, *Spoon River Anthology*.

THOMAS MCGRATH (1918–   )
Born on a North Dakota farm. Has published seven volumes of poetry, including *Figures from a Double World; Letters to an Imaginary Friend*; and *New and Selected Poems* (1964).

GEORGE MEREDITH (1828–1909)
Born in Portsmouth, England. Novelist, poet, editor. His novels include *The Egoist, Richard Feverel, Diana of the Crossways*. He wrote more than eight volumes of poems.

EDNA ST. VINCENT MILLAY (1892–1950)
Born in Rockland, Maine. Received a B.A. from Vassar College in 1917, the year in which her first volume of verse, *Renascence and Other Poems*, appeared. She was awarded the Pulitzer Prize in 1923.

NHAT-HANH, THICH (20th Century)
Vietnamese Bhuddist scholar and poet. Author of *Vietnam: Lotus in a Sea of Fire* (1967).

WILFRED OWEN (1893–1918)
Born in England. Enlisted in the Artists' Rifles in 1915; was awarded the M.C. and killed in action, 1918. His poems were first collected in 1920 by Siegfried Sassoon.

TOM PAXTON (1937–)
Born in Chicago. Composer, author, folk singer.

ROBERT PETERSON (1924–)
Born in Denver, Colorado. Author of *Home for the Night* (1962).

PO CHU-I (772–846)
Chinese poet of the T'ang Dynasty.

EDGAR ALLAN POE (1809–49)
Poet and critic, master of the short story, visionary of the anti-world, creator of a literature of mystery.

PETER PORTER (1929–)
He comes from Brisbane and has lived in London since 1951. He has published two books of poems, *Once Bitten, Twice Bitten* and *Poems Ancient and Modern*.

EZRA POUND (1895–)
Born in Hailey, Idaho, of New England stock. He was a founder of the Imagist movement, helped create an audience for Japanese drama and Chinese poetry in England and America, and influenced the careers of Joyce, Eliot, Tagore, and others.

FRANCIS QUARLES (1592–1644)
Trained in the law; one of the most unique of the religious poets of the 17th century.

SIR WALTER RALEIGH (1552?–1618)
Besides being statesman, courtier, soldier, and explorer, Raleigh distinguished himself as occasional poet.

JOHN CROWE RANSOM (1888–)
Born in Pulaski, Tennessee. Principal works: *Chills and Fever* (1924); *The New Criticism* (1941); *Selected Poems* (1945).

HERBERT READ (1893–1966)
Born in Yorkshire, England. Distinguished critic of art and literature as well as a poet. His *Collected Poems* appeared in 1966.

EDWIN ARLINGTON ROBINSON (1869–1935)
Born in Head Tide, Maine. His reputation was fully established with *The Man Against the Sky* in 1916. A winner of the Pulitzer Prize three times, today he is an important but much neglected poet.

MARGARET ROCKWELL (20th Century)

The poem "Hiroshima" appeared in *Theme and Variations, an Anthology* (1958).

W. R. RODGERS (1911–   )

Born in Ulster and educated at Queen's University, Belfast. His collection of verse, *Awake! and other poems*, was published in 1941.

THEODORE ROETHKE (1908–63)

Born in Saginaw, Michigan. A poet superior in his craft, his last book, *Words for the Wind* (1959), won three national awards.

EDWIN ROLFE (1909–   )

Born in Philadelphia. His books of poems include *To My Contemporaries* and *First Love*. He is also a writer of mystery novels and short stories.

SIEGFRIED SASSOON (1886–1967)

Educated at Marlborough and Clare College, Cambridge. Served in World War I. He made his reputation by his war poems.

F. R. SCOTT (1899–   )

Born in Quebec city. A moving spirit in the contemporary poetry of Canada. Has published four books of poetry: *Overture* (1945), *Events and Signals* (1954), *The Eye of the Needle* (1957), and *Signature* (1964).

JOHN SCOTT OF AMWELL (1730–83)

Born in England. A Quaker, among his works are *Four Moral Eclogues* (1778), *Observations on the State of the Parochial and Vagrant Poor* (1773).

WILLIAM SHAKESPEARE (1564–1616)

The lines quoted from *King Lear* and *Henry V* show Shakespeare, as always, concerned with the human situation, whether the man be king or commoner.

PERCY BYSSHE SHELLEY (1792–1822)

Born in Sussex. Eloquent defender of personal freedom and champion of the poet "as the unacknowledged legislator of the world."

JAMES SHIRLEY (1596–1666)

English dramatist, born in London. He was a prolific writer for the stage and wrote more than thirty plays. He produced four small volumes of poetry between 1646 and 1649.

STEVIE SMITH (1902–   )

A Londoner, the author of eight books of poems and drawings, three novels, and the recipient of the Cholmondeley Award for Poetry 1966.

WILLIAM JAY SMITH (1918–   )

Born in Louisiana. A Rhodes Scholar in 1947. His books of poetry include *Poems* and *Celebration at Dark*. He presently teaches at Williams College.

STEPHEN SPENDER (1909–   )

Educated at University College School, London, and University

College, Oxford; made his poetic reputation in the thirties. Was inspired by left-wing political sympathies, but his subsequent work is personal rather than political.

GEORGE STARBUCK (1931–)
Born in Ohio. He is the author of *Bone Thoughts* (1960) and *White Paper* (1966).

YURI SUHL (1908–)
Born in Poland; came to America in 1923. He has published four volumes of poetry in Yiddish and two novels in English.

JONATHAN SWIFT (1667–1745)
Born in Dublin of English parents. His verse is satiric and often informed with his fierce hatred of civilized sham.

ALFRED, LORD TENNYSON (1809–82)
Both for good and for ill, he was the voice of Victorian England.

DYLAN THOMAS (1914–53)
Distinguished himself as a broadcaster; wrote poems, stories, essays, and fragments of autobiography. His *Collected Poems* appeared in 1952.

TS'AO SUNG, CHINESE (c. 870–920)
Read in the shadow of the war in Vietnam, this early Chinese poem suggests how little man has learned from the ravages of war.

ROBERT TUCKER (1921–)
Born in New Hampshire. Served in the Marine Corps in World War II. Poet, outstanding teacher of writing at the University of Massachusetts. Has published poetry and fiction.

HENRY VAUGHAN (1621–95)
Born in Wales. Studied law, but later studied medicine and became a successful country doctor. Of the metaphysical poets, he is compared to George Herbert and John Donne.

CHAD WALSH (1914–)
Born in Virginia. On the English faculty of Beloit College. Poet and anthologist, his most recent book is the anthology *The Honey and the Gall*, poems of married life.

WANG TSAN (177–217)
In the poem "War in Chang-an City" the poet was indirectly showing his disapproval of the Emperor Wu, whose warmaking had plunged the country into misery.

EDWARD WARD (1667–1731)
English satirist and pub keeper. The author of *The London Spy* (1698–1700), a forerunner of the *Tatler* and *Spectator* papers.

RICHARD WEBER (1932–)
Born in Dublin, Ireland. Has published four volumes of poetry and his poems have appeared in numerous anthologies. His latest book of poems is *Lady & Gentleman* (1963).

SAMUEL WESLEY (1766–1837)
Born in England. Greatest organist of his day, classical scholar, prolific composer.

WALT WHITMAN (1819–92)

Born on Long Island, New York, Whitman was the new, democratic voice called for by Emerson in his essay "The Poet."

REED WHITTEMORE (1919–   )

Born in New Haven, Connecticut. The author of *Heroes and Heroines* (1946) and *An American Takes a Walk* (1956).

JOHN GREENLEAF WHITTIER (1807–92)

Quaker and protester, the anti-slavery poet of America.

WILLIAM WORDSWORTH (1770–1850)

Born in Cumberland in the English lake district. With Samuel Taylor Coleridge, ushered in the Romantic movement, 1798.

WILLIAM BUTLER YEATS (1865–1939)

Along with T. S. Eliot and Ezra Pound, was one of the shapers of the modern poetic tradition.